D1337186

The Electrics Come to Clachan

SYBIL ARMSTRONG

The Electrics Come to Clachan

Illustrated by the author

HUTCHINSON OF LONDON

Hutchinson & Co. (Publishers) Ltd
3 Fitzroy Square, London WIP 6JD

London Melbourne Sydney Auckland
Wellington Johannesburg and agencies
throughout the world

First published 1979

© Sybil Armstrong 1979

Set in Monotype Bembo

Printed in Great Britain by The Anchor Press Ltd
and bound by Wm Brendon & Son Ltd
both of Tiptree, Essex

British Library CIP data
Armstrong, Sybil
The electrics come to Clachan
1. Clachan, Scot. – Social life and customs
I. Title
941.1′72   DA890.C55

ISBN 0 09 139030 3

Contents

1

The peewits' storm

Spring had come again to Clachan and we were basking in the bright but somewhat tepid sunshine of April – less warm on this particular morning than it might have been because of the chilly wind blowing from the north-west. This fine weather could change extremely quickly up here, so we enjoyed the sun and the lovely colours that it painted everything; at the same time we would remember that an icy wind from the direction of *this* one *could* mean queer weather in the offing.

At Clachan, though, we were so used to battling with the elements that we took it all as it came and never allowed it to bother us. We wore clothing suitable for these parts and we all knew the do's and don'ts regarding our poultry and croft animals during rough weather, and it was of no use bothering ourselves about what we knew we were going to be treated to.

Clachan, perched above the estuary of our twelve-mile-long sea-loch, was surrounded by high mountains – all dipping their feet into the waters of the loch. The village consisted of a dozen or so white-washed croft-houses, each one's croft descending steeply to the loch shore. The Minch, joined by the waters of our loch below the brae on which our croft-houses stood, lay between the mainland of the north-west Scottish Highlands and the long faint line of misty blue, the Hebrides, which we could see on a fine day. On this particular morning this treacherous stretch of water, gorgeously painted gentian blue and apple-green in the sunlight, was being whipped up by the wind to drive masses of white wave-crests in towards the coast.

More and higher breakers, as the gale became more fierce, hurtled into our loch estuary, to crash in clouds of white spume thirty or forty feet high on the rocky cliffs a mile away on the opposite headland.

I had come to live in Clachan directly my war job finished, in 1945, and the small community – all Gaelic-speaking – were friendly right from the start, and as I was absolutely green regarding the running of a croft when I came, they had always been most helpful.

Life up here was completely different to the one I'd been used to before, but having no amenities was worth putting up with just to be away from noise and traffic – annoyances which the Clachan people had never had to experience. Most of them were bilingual and could speak English very well, but not all, so when I, who at that time knew no Gaelic to speak of, met up with one of the purely Gaelic-speaking crofters or their wives we had to resort to miming, and usually ended our efforts in laughter.

I had brought Corrie, my spaniel, with me; the rest of the menagerie – all of them poultry and animals necessary for the running of a croft – trickled into my possession at various periods during the four years that I had lived in Clachan. Little had changed here since I came, and methods and customs remained for the most part as they had been in the time of the present crofters' grandparents.

As the morning on this April day advanced, the wind increased to gale force; the sky clouded over, and it was evident that rain was near. In the ordinary way none of us would think anything of this; crofters are accustomed to going out in all weathers. But at this time of the year it was different. It was now lambing-time, and each year at this time didn't we have a freak storm, long after the real winter snow had gone from the braes?

This storm was always preceded by strong winds, heavy rain and hail, the hailstones often being as big as marbles, and it was called 'the peewits' storm', for the peewits, or lapwings, always returned about now after their winter absence.

Kirsty, my nearest neighbour in her croft along the track, had told me about it the first year I had come up here. 'And so soon as yourself sees the thick black clouds coming up beyond yon mountains,' she had said, 'hurry and fetch your cows in from the brae, whateffer, for the hailstones tear the hides of the domestic cattle, although it doesna seem to hurt the shaggy Highland breed, for their hides are thicker and covered more heavily with hair. . . .'

On this morning, then, my cows were a good way up the brae when I noticed the inky-black clouds gathering and I made a dash up there to fetch them down, but the raindrops started falling before I reached Geal, Bess and friends. With luck, though, I thought we might get down to the byre before the hail started. Beth, my neighbour on the other side down the track, came tearing out of her croft-house, waved, and arrived beside the cows – hers being with mine – at the same time as I did. We drove them all down together, Beth and I exchanging bits of conversation with difficulty while we bent forward against the rain, now coming down like stair-rods, the wind roaring through the mountains. And did you ever try to get a cow to amble along more quickly? Believe me, there are few things that can be more totally impossible! I moaned to Beth about the weather and felt a worm because Beth never moaned about anything. She took everything as it came in her placid way, and what a lot of worry she saved herself! I wished so often that I could be like Beth. . . .

'Our usual lambing-time storm coming on, Beth, isn't it?'
I complained.

'Ay – the peewits' storm,' she shouted back. 'But herself'll
no' be lasting more than four days at the most, whateffer.'

'And meanwhile lots of birds sitting on eggs – dotted around
on the brae – will be buried right there, where they're sitting!'
I bawled.

'Ach yes, indeed, it is so. But it never seems to make any
difference. There are chust as many next year, whateffer. . . .'

She went on to shout some news. 'Seumas' – her husband –
'has driven the Laird into Inverness the day, to meet that niece
of his off the train from the south, whateffer.' Seumas worked
down at Craig House, about thirteen miles away. He was a
chauffeur-cum-under-factor to the Laird as Dugald, the latter's
son, had married Trudy, my niece, and gone to live in the
States. So in Dugald's place now there were the new factor and
Seumas. Aunt Annabel, as she preferred everyone to call her,
who had stepped into the breech when Lady MacConnach,
Dugald's mother, had died, continued to keep house, and everything ran very smoothly. Still, I did find myself wondering
how this niece, straight from boarding school, would get on
with Aunt Annabel – a much-respected old lady, but one who
disliked 'modern' *anything*!

'Is the girl's father dead, too, that she's coming all this way
north to live?' I asked Beth, who was bound to know.

'Oh ay. According to the Laird himself, the lassie – Seumas
thought "Carol" was her name – had no one but her relatives up
here, whateffer.'

It was too difficult trying to carry on a conversation in the
rain and boisterous wind, so Beth waved her hand and drove
her cows off to her byre and Geal, Bess and I continued on our
way over the heather hummocks and rush-clumps. When we
reached the track I almost bumped into Fearchar Psalms and
Kenny Mor, two elderly crofters who lived at the far end of the

village. My cows, knowing their way, continued along the track on their own to the open gate and on up to the byre while I stopped for a moment to speak to the two men who, backs to the gale, had stopped too and were wiping their rain-dripping brows and lashes with enormous coloured handkerchiefs. Fearchar wore his soaking cloth cap and ancient black oilskin coat which he swore still kept him dry, and Kenny had on the chic little number we all knew so well – an almost prehistoric black overcoat and his cloth cap, and all dripping wet. But Kenny had taken the precaution against getting his neck wet by tucking his lush, white, Father Christmas beard inside the top of his coat. Older Clachanites remembered that Kenny had possessed a lovely yellow oilskin coat; but unfortunately he'd hung it on a rowan tree in his front garden to drip-dry, and some cows ambling down from the brae saw it, ate it (they adore linseed), and left nothing for Kenny to collect but the press-studs and belt-buckle!

Fearchar hailed me in his usual voice, which was like something breaking the sound barrier.

'The peewits' storm, whateffer!' he bawled. 'Ourselves are chust making our way to the post office before the weather gets any worse!'

And Kenny butted in with: 'Would yourself be all right for stamps, mistress? Or will we be bringing you some on our way back?'

'I'm all right for them, thanks, Kenny,' I shouted back, 'but would you mind bringing my mail – if there is any?'

'Ourselves'll do that, certainly,' replied Kenny gravely, stiff as a poker so that his beard wouldn't get dislodged.

'And where's your trio?' yelled Fearchar. The 'trio' were my three inseparables – Corrie, my spaniel; Tee-tee, the half-wild cat; and Tòmas, a black Shetland lamb who had lived with us as the third part of the 'trio' since the day he arrived in the world – his mother was a victim of a dreadful dog-worry-ing episode last year and he was left an orphan.

'They started out with me, Fearchar,' I shouted back, 'but didn't like the rain and went home.'

'Ach – themselves knew fine where it was warm and com-fortable,' he grinned. 'And,' he went on, bellowing louder than ever, 'yourself would no' be having a cup of tea at a loose end, no knowing what to do with itself, as we came back, would you?' Fearchar was a real old woman for his cups of tea, which always seemed to taste better if he had someone to talk to while he drank them.

'I'll have one ready when you come back,' I grinned, waving as I hurried into the yard. The two over-seventies went on their way, bent double against the storm, while I, after giving the cows hay and water, got myself into my warm kitchen as quickly as I could, and put the kettle on to boil. The trio barely roused themselves even when I stirred the fire, making it crackle and send out myriads of tiny sparks. . . .

Fearchar and Kenny duly arrived, bringing me my mail. Their dripping coats and caps hung up, they came into the kitchen mopping their faces and drew chairs up to the fire, blazing merrily. Fearchar asked me if I'd heard the news.

'About the Laird's niece coming to live at Craig House?' I asked.

'Ay – the Laird told Seumas yesterday that he was sure her-self was a nice lassie, but that he'd been told that she was a young lady who liked to be doing something all the time – being busy like. And himself said: "She works hard, but she likes to play hard too", and I'm thinking mysel' that there's no' much going on here in the way of "play", hard or no'! But both Seumas and myself were wondering chust what the Laird meant by "*play* hard"?'

I explained as best I could, but it wasn't easy; in this part of

Scotland we all had to stick pretty closely to the working of our crofts and caring for our livestock, so there was little time for play, hard or otherwise. And, of course, in a remote place like Clachan – all steep mountainsides – there was no ground level enough to play any of the ordinary games played in other parts – tennis, shinty, football or even golf. Although the scenery up here was truly 'out of this world', it wasn't by admiring the scenery that we could keep ourselves. For instance, the subsoil was very shallow, and it was stony and steep, so we had to work hard to grow our crops, and we hadn't much time for leisure; but the peace and quiet up here was appreciated by all of us. A crofter was his own boss, too.

Still, we had to be prepared to have in exchange little leisure time, no public transport and no amenities. Kirsty shrewdly pointed out on several occasions in my hearing, 'Ourselves must no' be having the track repaired whateffer, or sure's death it would allow the tourists to come here – and then where would Clachan be with bottles and papers and cigarette cartons scattered all over the place? No, no. Let ourselves stay quiet and happy chust, and be as we are. . . .'

So our four-mile track stayed as it was, potholes and all. And of the Clachan people, the men were quite content with their Saturday evening 'leisure' – all they allowed themselves excepting for the Sabbath, when apart from looking after the animals, most of the rest of the day was spent in church or in walking to or coming from it; but on Saturdays they cycled the twelve miles down to Craig Hotel whatever the weather, for a few wee drams with friends, and bought their Black Twist tobacco for the coming week. Then they cycled the twelve miles back, along the switchback road all the way and often in the pitch darkness – with the sheep lying all over the roadway. But you never heard a moan about that.

As for the women, they had even less leisure, and had to be

satisfied with the occasional half an hour with a neighbour for a cup of tea and a 'bit gossip'.

In the winter months there were the *ceilidhs* that Kirsty threw at her house, to which we all looked forward. On these occasions the *ceilidhs* never started until after nine, so that everyone could finish their work first. But they were nice and friendly, cosy and chatty, and very enjoyable for people who seldom had any entertainment at all – and nobody left for home until the 'wee sma' hours'. But now I wondered to myself how Carol would like *ceilidhs*. Would she care for the legend-telling, the singing of the old Gaelic working songs, and the 'shop' talk that went on to do with our crofts and our animals?

'I wonder what our newcomer looks like?' I said as I poured out more tea all round on this stormy morning.

'Ach well. Ourselves can no' be telling that until we see her, whateffer,' replied Fearchar philosophically, as he took a bite of his scone.

'And herself's chust seventeen!' informed Kenny. 'A child chust.'

'A *child*, Kenny?' I cried. 'At seventeen they wouldn't like to hear themselves called children nowadays!'

'Why?'

'Well, because they're quite grown-up long before then,' I said.

Kenny stopped eating his scone and stared at me. 'Really?' he queried.

'Indeed, yes,' put in Fearchar. 'I see them coming into the hotel when I work there in the summer. 'Deed, they're quite grown-up at seventeen. And I'm hoping the lassie'll no' be wearin' the throwser, like so many of them do!' he said as though he meant it.

Kenny burst out laughing.

'Ach – what if she does? She's doing no harm – '

'Is she no'?' bawled Fearchar in his sergeant-major voice. 'Let them do what they like anywhere else, whateffer; but no' in Clachan. Here, we're wantin' nothin' altered – and we're no' wantin' women wearin' the throwser here!'

'And ourselves can be doing nothing about it if she does!' tittered old Kenny.

I felt myself going purple and more purple, for I'd never forgotten the day soon after I'd arrived in Clachan when, it being a really chilly day, I'd donned a pair of slacks for extra warmth and had run into Fearchar along the track. He tore me off such a strip that I'd slunk home and changed into a skirt before appearing in public again; after that even when the gale felt as though it were coming straight from the Arctic, I've never dared to wear slacks again in Clachan!

Fearchar, his tea and scones finished, dived into a capacious pocket for his pipe, took it out, filled it, lit it, spat accurately at a flame in the fire and began puffing clouds of Black Twist all over us. He looked extremely happy, and soon Kenny followed Fearchar's example. After a little while, though, I was sad at having to disturb the two men and their smoke dreams, I simply had to feed the animals. They knew the time quite as well as we humans did, and I tried to keep as nearly as possible to the times they were used to having their meals.

I got up. 'Now, you two go on sitting by the fire, will you?' I said, 'but I must get these mashes and things round – '

Fearchar instantly came to.

'You'll do no such thing!' he shouted. 'Myself and Kenny will be doing that for you. And after that ourselves will be on our way – '

At that moment the hail began coming down like millions of tons of pebbles being emptied on to the corrugated iron roof, and what with that and the gale the noise was so awful we couldn't have heard ourselves speak, and the men didn't try. They made signs intimating to me that they'd take the stuff round as soon as the hail stopped, and once more sat down by the fire to wait, while I busied myself preparing the midday feeds for the croft animals.

The elderly men were very old friends, who each lived alone in a croft-house near the other, at the far end of the village. They were both bachelors, and although very good friends in the real sense – e.g. caring for each other's stock if either had to be out – their temperaments differed considerably.

Fearchar was a decided extrovert, enjoying every moment of his life to the full. He had several jobs which for the most part kept him quite busy, for besides his own croft and croft livestock to keep going, he was Precentor at the little Kirk down the lochside. The services were all in Gaelic – the language spoken ordinarily up here – and Fearchar would stand facing the congregation arrayed in his 'Sunday Blacks' and an outsize pair of spotlessly white gloves, holding up his open book of the psalms. When the minister announced the psalm – hymns weren't sung up here, only psalms – Fearchar would burst out a most impressive and somewhat deafening 'first line', so that everyone could come in on the same key. He was also one of the church elders, and at the *ceilidhs* he was our champion legend-teller. Any spare time he had was spent either in doing any odd jobs anyone wanted done – for which he always refused to be paid – or in making really professional-looking shepherds' crooks from blackthorn gathered from a spot where they grew several miles inland, and horn from deceased ewes or rams. These sold well either at the little hotel tourist shop which had been started last year, or in the markets on the east coast, when Fearchar could get anyone to take them in for him. In spite of the fact that he was over seventy he, like so many men around here, was even in his old age over six feet tall, and as straight and upright as anyone half his age. His iron-grey hair was still thick, and he possessed a most luxuriant walrus moustache the same colour; his eyes were blue – not quite so blue now as they had once been – and his cheery face, leathery and rather red, told of a life spent mostly out of doors.

Kenny Mor – 'Big Kenny' – had an entirely different disposition to Fearchar's. Kenny was quieter, and, although he would quite conscientiously do essential chores in the house and on the croft, he would prefer to sit dreaming by his peat-fire, or go out for a stroll, or even snooze off in the warm kitchen; he wasn't one for working at anything he didn't have to, and his pet aversion was running a garden, as opposed to growing his crops. Kirsty had badgered him into making himself a vegetable garden near the croft-house at the back, but he only attended to this as a concession to Kirsty, who hated to see an inch of ground wasted that could be put to some useful purpose. Kenny's hair, beard, moustache and eyebrows were snow-white, and he was a very good-looking old man, and, like Fearchar, he'd always do anything to help anyone.

It would have been a real curse to Kenny to have kept his small front garden going with fruit trees that needed pruning and flowers that needed sowing or planting each year, like Kirsty's; or with extra vegetables, like Beth and Seumas's; but nature solved that one for him. Four years ago Kenny had been to stay with his married sister's family in Inverness, and the lovely golden star-shaped flowers of the St John's Wort in her garden gave him an idea. She had complained to him that the plant had to be kept down, 'cut ruthlessly back' in other words, or it would take over. How wonderful, Kenny thought, if it took over his front garden in Clachan! So he brought some cuttings home with him, and the only pruning he'd had to do since then was to cut a path through it to his gate!

2

Carol visits Clachan

The next morning a white blanket covered the mountain-tops and the braes. The peewits' storm was truly with us again. Once the snow was all down, however, we neither felt, saw, nor heard any more of the storm. Although it hadn't lasted long, and everyone had known that in two or three days we'd be back to normal again, it was always enough to disorganize things considerably. The tiny newborn lambs couldn't go on the brae with their mothers when there was snow, and mothers and babies had to be kept sheltered in pens which were bound to be limited in space. Newly hatched chicks had to be kept in, cattle, too, and horses. Many of the wild birds nesting on the braes when the snow suddenly arrived again were buried where they sat. It was skiddy and dangerous trying to take a car or bike along the Highland switchback roads – hardly any of which were banked, and practically all of which had precipices on one side.

Then when the thaw came hundreds of new little burns cascaded down the mountainsides. But these, given a burst of good weather and no more snow or rain for a day or two, would disappear as quickly as they began.

Beth and her husband Seumas called in the evening, on their way to spend an odd hour with Kirsty. Seumas had driven the

Laird to Inverness three days before, but until last night the storm had persisted so nobody had any news other than that of the arrival of the Laird's niece at Craig House. Beth persuaded me to go along to Kirsty's with them. The old lady was always delighted to see any of us in the late evenings, when our work was finished for the day. She couldn't work now as she used to do on the croft, so her married daughter, Anna, who lived in the next croft-house past Kirsty's own, used to cope with the lighter work on both crofts, and the men, Alastair, Kirsty's son, and Gregor, her son-in-law, would carry on with the heavier work in the evenings when they came home from their ordinary day's work. Kirsty herself was plump and had wavy silvery hair, and slightly faded blue eyes, and she was blessed with a cheery, hospitable disposition; she was greatly respected and adored by everyone around the lochside, and those farther afield, too.

As soon as we arrived at her house she put the kettle on to boil, and we drew chairs up to the fire. After talking 'shop' for a little, the subject inevitably came round to Carol, the Laird's niece – for, up here, any new arrival was hot news.

'And now, Seumas,' said Kirsty, 'since you're the only one among us who's seen the young lady – what like is herself?'

'Ach – a nice lassie, whateffer,' was the reply.

'Ay – but will she be good-looking or –'

'Well, no' bad-looking at all, Kirsty. You'll wish me to describe herself for you?' queried Seumas.

'Ay,' Kirsty smiled, settling herself comfortably in her armchair, Beth having said she'd see to the tea. 'Well, her eyes – what colour are they?'

'Ach well. I'd say they were greenish. They kind o' glowed – green.'

'It's no' "glowed", Seumas,' corrected Beth in a stage whisper which could have been heard over on the other side of the loch. She liked to get things right. 'Shone.'

'And it's no "shone", either,' Seumas barked back. 'Whisht, woman!' At that Beth poured out the tea, then sat up very straight and began to knit furiously, but apart from these indications of her annoyance we knew she'd never pursue the subject further, although it *was* a bit galling to be told to 'whisht!' before other people. She seemed to cringe right back into her shell like a scared winkle, and Seumas again held the floor.

'Ay, themselves are greenish all right,' he said.

Kirsty was interested in this 'greenish' colour. Up here, eyes were always blue or brown, and she'd never heard of green eyes.

'Well,' she bristled, 'supposing you tell us what like were her eyes really, Seumas?' Obviously she didn't believe him.

'Green,' stated Seumas flatly, 'and her hair's chestnut –'

'Auburn,' breathed Beth ever so softly, knitting very fast.

No one took any notice, and Seumas continued: 'Ach – she's a nice enough lassie; but I'd say she mostly gets what she wants. Well, well. And herself was telling me that she's heard about Kirsty from her uncle, and wants to come up here to Clachan and meet her.'

Kirsty smiled happily.

'Ach – that'll be nice – and myself'll phone Aunt Annabel, too. When would be the best time to ask them to tea, Seumas – and it'll have to be soon, because we'll be starting on the spring-work –'

And so the talk went on, until the chat lengthened into an hour, then Beth got up and Seumas and I followed suit. We said good-bye to Kirsty and walked along together, parting company at my gate. Seumas had to make another hen-coop that night, he said, before he went to bed – and I knew he had to leave for his work at Craig House by six in the morning. And Craig House was thirteen miles away!

In four days' time dawned the Sabbath. There were no more signs of the peewits' storm. It might never have happened. I took the meals and mashes round and had my breakfast, then about ten I got ready to do the milking. The Clachan people, wearing their 'Sunday Blacks,' had mostly set off on their ten-mile walk to the Kirk by then. A bit later, the milking done, I was carrying the buckets of milk to the dairy when I heard the clatter of hoofs coming my way along the track.

The next thing I knew, rider and horse had pulled up at my gate. Looking in that direction I saw a smart young lady on the mare that I was sure was the Laird's. Dumping the buckets inside the dairy, I closed the door and went to see what this unusual Sabbath visit was in aid of.

'Oh, hullo!' called the smiling girl from her perch aloft. 'Would you be Miss Armstrong?'

'Yes,' I replied with an attempt at a welcoming smile, though I knew that this Sabbath visit would not go unnoticed, and in fact would be regarded by the Clachan people as beyond the pale. And what was more, I also knew that I might expect a reproach from the church elders for encouraging this young miss in profaning the Sabbath by not ordering her immediately to about-turn and go home. For I knew that it must be Carol, though I hadn't seen her before. And to make matters worse, Carol was 'wearin' the throwser', at which Fearchar would be furious and the elderly members of the community shocked. Oh, well, if they wanted to be funny about this escapade or whatever, that was their business. It was nothing to do with me, and I, at any rate, intended to make her feel welcome. But how extraordinary, I thought, that the Laird should lend his niece his mare to ride on the Sabbath! In fact, he'd never been known to lend the mare to *anyone*. . . .

'I'm Carol Burnett,' my caller told me, her auburn hair glinting gloriously in the sunlight, for she wasn't wearing a hat. 'Can I come in and chat to you for a few minutes?'

'Yes, of course,' I answered. 'I'll be delighted. Just follow me, and when we've stabled the mare we'll go into the house and have some coffee.'

'That would be *super!*' she exclaimed, following me to the stable, where she dismounted, saw to the mare, and came across to the house. In the kitchen, which we all looked upon as the drawing room, she sat down with a sigh of relief.

'My, but it's chilly today!' she smiled, giving a little shiver as she held out her hands to the fire.

'Well, there's still quite a cold wind blowing, isn't there?' I grinned, fussing with the coffee. 'But I just can't think how you got away with – what you *have* got away with!'

'Get away with what?' It was the girl's turn to be surprised.

'Well,' I began lamely, hardly knowing how to begin. How was I going to tackle this business about the Clachan attitude to Sunday, to someone who was obviously ignorant of having put her foot in it?

'Carol,' I began, 'in this part of Scotland the people are rather puritanical – ultra religious, let's say – and they don't go anywhere on Sunday except to church. And *I* know, because I fell by the wayside several times when I first came up here! You'll get used to it, I do assure you; still, I think it was easier for me to stick to the rules about the Sabbath up here than it might be for you because – well, I was so tired at the end of a full week's hard work on the croft that I was glad of a restful day, and that part of it didn't worry me at all!'

'So what you're trying to tell me is that I'll be for ever damned for riding – up here – on a Sunday?' She helped herself to another scone.

'No reproof from me, anyway. Far from it,' I answered. 'I'm only trying to put you wise to customs prevalent up here. They'll know *you* didn't know, but they'll wonder why the Laird didn't put you wise to it. That's his mare, isn't it? I'd have thought he'd have told you – '

Carol's face went very red.

'Oh – but he doesn't know I've taken the mare!' she muttered.

Well, I wasn't going to lecture the girl about taking the lovely, glossy Raineach that the Laird had his groom care for like a bit of Dresden china; let 'himself' argue things out with her when she got back – and she'd better try to get back without the family seeing her as they came out of church. But it wasn't my business, anyway – and Carol was so newly up here that surely the Laird would turn a blind eye for this once?

'That's yours and your uncle's business, Carol,' I pointed out. 'As far as I'm concerned it's simply marvellous to have you – Sunday or any other day, and you'll get just the same welcome from Jean-Post-Office, I do assure you – '

'Jean-Post-Office? Who's that?'

'The other person from the south. Somebody must have told you about us,' I queried, 'because you knew where I lived – '

'Oh, yes. On the way back from Inverness in the car,' she said, 'my uncle told me there were two ladies from the south living here, and coming along today I passed an old man with a long white beard, and I asked him which was your house – '

'That would be Kenny Mor,' I said. 'He can't walk to the Kirk so he stays behind and looks after several people's young stock while they've gone.'

'Well, I'd made up my mind I was going to get up here to see you somehow. My uncle had taken the Daimler when he and Aunt Annabel went to church or I'd have borrowed that – '

'For goodness' sake, Carol,' I cried. 'There'd have been hell to pay if you had!'

'Why?'

'Well. . . . But did you just take what you wanted to borrow, without asking first, when you lived in the south?'

'At home I did. There were certain things at school we

could borrow without asking, too – the horses, for instance, in our time off. And at home, well, I just took the car if I wanted it.' She drank some coffee, and went on: 'Well, whatever happens through my taking Uncle's mare, apart from the sin I've committed by coming to visit anybody on Sunday, you and Jean-Post-Office'll let me come to see you sometimes, won't you? I feel I'll burst if I don't let my hair down sometimes, at any rate until I get more accustomed to being terribly good, which it seems I'll have to be at Craig House, and I feel it in my bones that you two will understand.'

I nodded. 'Of course we'll understand,' I said with a grin. 'You come up here and have a chat and a cuppa whenever you like. If you don't see me around, I'll likely be right down the croft by the shore; or you could go along to Jean. . . . She's in all the time during the week, poor thing. *Has* to be! And I'll tell you someone else who'd understand – Kirsty. When you've finished your elevenses we'll walk along and see Jean, and perhaps we'll have a few minutes to spare to call in and introduce you to Kirsty.'

'That's gorgeous of you! Now I'll know I've got a few friends not far away, and I feel much happier. But wait. . . . How in the world am I going to get here without walking the thirteen miles, or without borrowing some sort of transport?'

'I'll tell you how,' I said. 'You just phone Clachan post office and tell Jean you want to come up here. She'll come along and tell me, and I'll nip down and fetch you in Myrtle – '

'Myrtle?'

'My little Austin Seven.'

'Oh, thanks. That'll be super! I'll be getting a car myself as soon as death duties and things are all settled. I *can* drive.'

'Well, that's fine,' I said, 'and until then we'll help about your getting here.'

She remained quiet, thinking hard, for a minute or two;

then she said: 'If the people here are a bit sticky about human beings doing this and that on Sundays, how do the animals come off?'

'Oh – looking after the croft animals is an exception. Crofters couldn't be crofters in a remote place like this without their animals and poultry. So they're all cared for in the same way as they are on any other day. And I'll tell you something. I doubt very much whether anyone would expect Nurse to call a doctor – our nearest lives thirty miles away – on a Sunday, and of course a vet would be "out" too, seeing he also would have a long way to come, and on a Sunday. But one of the crofters over at Ros, opposite, had something wrong with one of his cows and he *did* actually send for the vet on the Sabbath – and this man had to come out all the way from Inverness, and, of course, it wasn't only the motor journey, but also meant going over to Ros in a boat from Clachan. So that little episode has gone down in Clachan's history. But it goes to show that they care very much for their animals, doesn't it? And just the same on Sundays, too,' I finished up.

'It certainly does,' she agreed, munching some scone and washing it down with coffee. 'Does anyone ride horseback here? And are you the only one who drives a car – not counting the hotel people?'

'Well, as far as riding goes, I've only seen the Laird ride horseback latterly, although Dugald, when he was at home, used to do so. Plenty of people ride the Highland ponies, though, when they go up into the mountains after deer. And as for cars – several people around the lochside *can* drive, though hardly anyone has a car. Myrtle's the only car in Clachan, but I believe we may have some more in the near future because Beth and Peigi MacLennan – both living at Clachan – have asked me to teach them to drive, and I'm starting with Peigi this week.'

Carol had almost finished her elevenses, so I suggested we

went along to see Jean-Post-Office now. As we walked along
the track I asked Carol if she'd met any of the church people
on her way here.

'Masses of them!' she replied airily, 'and now I come to
think of it, they did look rather sideways at me!'

'Never mind. They'll know you didn't know, I'm sure. . . .
And you say the Laird and Aunt Annabel both went to church
this morning, then?'

'Yes, they both went. They said I wouldn't understand a
word of the service because it was all in Gaelic. But I'm afraid
I didn't suggest that I should go along with them and just *sit*.
I had the idea that I'd come up here and try to find you, you
see?'

'Well, I'm very glad we've met, Carol. When I first came
up here I was excused attending the church services, too,
because they were in Gaelic, and, of course, I didn't know any!
I wasn't broken-hearted though, frankly, because I didn't
much relish the ten-mile walk there and back that they all do
without a moan. I think the Clachan people are noble to do it.'

'So do I. Have you learnt Gaelic now?'

'Well, only a few sentences of it, I'm afraid. After a hard
day's crofting one doesn't feel all that much inclined to swot!
At least, I haven't felt like keeping it up. But I'm always
promising myself – and Kirsty – that I will some day. . . .'

There wasn't a soul about, of course, as we walked along,
and Carol remarked that everyone might have been dead in
the place! At the post office gate we went in and up the path,
and Carol asked if we just walked in.

'Yes, lift the doorlatch – '

'Hullo, Jean!' I called as we came in.

'Oh, hullo!' she replied. 'Take a pew, both of you. I'll make
a cup of coffee.'

'Thanks, but we've just had one, Jean. I've brought Carol
along to meet you. She's ridden from Craig – '

'*Ridden?*'

Carol nodded, going rather red, and Jean, sensing all was not going quite according to the rules and regs of Clachan, didn't pursue the subject, but went on: 'Well, I'm very pleased to meet you, Carol. One thing we three have in common is the fact that all of us have at some time lived in the south. The third part of this trio,' she continued, inclining her head in my direction, 'was my great friend in the south, and when I came up here to stay for a holiday I didn't want to go back – fell in love with the people, the scenery and the life up here, in other words; so when the then postmistress wanted to leave to get married, I applied for this job.'

'You see, Carol,' I put in, 'neither of us would like to live anywhere else in the world now – it grows on you up here, and it'll grow on you, too, I'm sure, when you get used to it.'

But, actually, I was very worried about that mare of the Laird's, and now I said: 'Carol – wouldn't it be a good idea just to give Craig House a tinkle while we're here, to say you and the mare are at Clachan? That's the only telephone, by the way – ' I nodded towards it on the wall. Jean thought it would be a good idea, too, and backed me up, though she hadn't the foggiest notion what we were talking about. A good scout, our Jean. . . .

'You think I ought?' the girl asked.

'I do, for I wouldn't mind betting there's a search-party out for you and the mare already!' The girl, muttering resignedly, went over to the phone, and Jean and I talked quietly while Carol carried on a conversation with the parlourmaid at Craig House.

In a few minutes she came back and sat down. 'Aunt Annabel and Uncle aren't back from church yet,' she said, 'and the parlourmaid doesn't think they will be for quite some time. But the search is apparently well and truly on, so it was as well that I phoned. The parlourmaid is going to rush out now to find the groom, who's been panic-stricken, it seems, about the mare!'

I'd managed to convey some details to Jean about Carol's visit in the few brief moments we had while Carol was phoning. The girl was lonely, I said, and it would be a good thing – and Jean agreed with me – to try to get her to see that she had friends to whom she could turn if the so-very-different life in the north-west Highlands got on top of her at any time. A pity we weren't nearer her own age, but we couldn't help that! Girls of Carol's age just didn't stay in places like this any more. They went to the towns, where there was something going on all the time.

We decided that Carol would do better today to try to get back to Craig House before the people came out of church. She agreed with us, and so we left sooner than we otherwise would have done. Jean pointed out that Kirsty, who couldn't do that long walk to church now, might have seen Carol and me pass, and would be expecting us to call, so we rushed in to see her. Fortunately Kirsty understood and agreed about Carol's trying to reach home before the family returned. Carol was delighted when Kirsty told her that she intended asking the younger element around the lochside to tea next Saturday, when she hoped Carol would be able to come too, to meet them.

The girl seemed genuinely pleased about it and confided to me that however cross the Laird was about the mare being borrowed without permission, it was worth all the row that was in store for her to know that now she wouldn't be feeling lonely and like a fish out of water any more, with her friends at Clachan.

As she saddled up and led Raineach out to the track, I said I'd keep my fingers crossed that she'd get past the Kirk before the people came out! Begging to come again soon, she mounted, waved, and cantered off along the verge at the side of the track.

Carol wasn't to be favoured with that bit of luck. Several of the black-arrayed men and women were coming down the little church path as she trotted by on the Laird's mare which, of course, as Carol herself knew, everyone would notice; but she hoped the family wasn't among those first people she saw coming out, and she hoped sincerely that she might manage to get back before her aunt and uncle.

About a mile past the church, though, she came to a spot where the rocks came right down to the road on either side and had to walk Raineach because of the loose stones that had rolled down the mountainsides as well as the fact that the road was narrower here. She eventually became aware of a car keeping behind her, for nothing could have passed at this place. She turned her head. It was the Daimler.

The crofthouse at Clachan

3

Diarmid to the rescue

Carol, who still underestimated the enormity of her misdeeds in a place where the two principal things in the people's lives were religion and crofting, waved her hand, and of course got no answering wave. As soon as the car could pass it did so, and pulled up in front of Raineach, blocking the way. The Laird, furious, hurried out of the driving seat and round to Carol and burst out angrily to his niece: 'And who told you you could take Raineach?'

The mare, glad to see him, rubbed her head affectionately against his chest and arm, and her master patted her glossy neck, which in places was showing signs of sweating, and this infuriated him more.

But he realized that this was no place for a brawl, and once Carol had replied to his question he'd reserve the rest of the scolding in store for her until they reached home.

'Nobody told me I could take Raineach,' she answered without hesitation. 'I didn't think you'd mind. . . . At school, you see, where we had fifteen horses for riding, we took whichever we fancied.'

'Well, we don't do things like that here, Carol,' her uncle fumed, 'and I do mind, very much.'

With that he walked quickly to the car, got into the driving seat, and in his anger exceeded the speed limit; luckily for him Iain-the-Police was many miles away in some far-flung part of his outsize beat. Aunt Annabel almost succumbed to an attack of the vapours, but clinging on to the seat with all her might, she closed her eyes and suffered in silence. And the Laird never slowed down until he began making his way up the drive to the house.

The stables were quite near, and here Aunt Annabel and he were waiting as Carol walked the mare up to one of the loose boxes. Knowing that she should walk her animal for the last part of the way before taking it in, she was not hurrying. 'And Uncle can't at least moan about that!' she thought, thanking Heaven.

Aunt Annabel didn't want to witness the row so the Laird took her arm and steered her into the house, and came back to Carol. He lost his temper and raged at her, and if Carol had been like the other women in his family, he reckoned when later on he came to think about it, she'd have burst into tears, and made things extremely awkward. But not Carol. She was made of sterner stuff, and would have had no hesitation in apologising for her misdeeds had she been able to get a word in. It was some time before that was possible; when it was, she thought it would be best in the circumstances to appear so contrite that she almost grovelled. This attitude couldn't have worked better on her uncle. It took his breath away, too, to think that she never tried to make any excuses.

The groom, Ewen, was hidden behind some bales of hay in one of the loose boxes, and he was, he confided to Cook later, absolutely stunned at the way the Laird buckled down and eventually accepted her apology; but for all that, Cook told him, she was rather sorry for Miss Carol, who must be finding everything vastly different to the life she'd known.

Lunch was quite the most awful meal Carol had ever experienced. Aunt Annabel reproached her on and off throughout the meal, and the Laird was still too angry to want to speak unless addressed by his sister. When they rose from the table the girl almost ran up to her bedroom, where she spent the rest of the afternoon wondering how in the world she was going to stick this sort of life, where religion and the customs and conventions seemed to be the principal things in her aunt's life; and the Laird, nice though Carol thought he was in the ordinary way, was more or less ruled by his sister. Carol was sure that everything she did would be wrong until she knew their funny ways up here – queer, of course, to her, because she had grown up believing that those she was accustomed to in the south would be 'standard' ones, where-ever she went.

In a couple of hours the gong went for tea, and though the girl would have given anything not to have had to go down-stairs for it, no meal, she told herself, could be worse than the last – and she'd got through that all right!

Evidently her aunt and uncle had decided during the after-noon that Carol's apologies were enough to put life on an even keel again, and, to the girl's relief, the matter was dropped. The conversation drifted into the ordinary channels again, even to the surprise of hearing Aunt Annabel suggesting to her brother that he should walk down to the hotel with Carol the next day to introduce her to Fiona and John. They were some of the younger set round here, and John and Dugald had been great friends before the latter married and went to live in America. Aunt Annabel was very fond of Fiona, so the couple were often to be seen at Craig House.

The next morning, as the Laird would be busy and his sister would be making butter, Carol suggested that she should take the dogs for a short walk in the mountains.

The Laird and Annabel both thought it a good idea, but cautioned her to keep to the paths – although they mostly didn't go on for much of a distance. She could turn round and come back then, couldn't she? And when the Laird had described what a bog looked like, so that she could avoid it, she and the Labradors started off on their walk. The mist-scarves around the tops were beginning to drift away and the sun looked like putting in an appearance; it did, and Carol was glad the weather was so good for her walk. *And* she'd managed to get away on her own into this exciting part of the world, so new to her, where she could try for a little while to forget her longing for the people and places she'd known before.

The snow had gone from the braes, but up on the tops the white blanket might stay for the summer months just as it was, right around to the time when more snow would fall, next winter. Once right in amongst the mountains like this, girl and dogs felt absolutely free, and Carol was amazed at the breath-taking views which opened up continually before her as she and the dogs scrambled over vast tracts of dead heather and masses of rush-clumps and round great boulders. And she reckoned she'd never seen a bluer sky. The white jagged summits were clear-cut against it, and she felt as if she'd been transported somehow into fairyland – the scenery even better than some of the lovely panoramic coloured picture-postcards she'd seen at times. Having long ago come to the end of the path she'd been following at first, she was still so obsessed that she just went on and on.

She entered a long, wide glen, bare except for the odd mass of dead heather, and only the word 'wild' could describe it. She was beginning to feel tired now, and sat down on a large stone to rest while the dogs went off on the scent of some animal. She looked around her: everywhere it was just glori-ously, incredibly, out of this world – the craggy rocks, the white uneven, jagged summits, all corrugated down their sides, and these all around her, the large tracts of dead heather and the huge boulders that had rolled down to the floor of the glen, where she was. The big burn that rushed through the middle of this glen – and on and on through a gap in the hills and down in a cascade – eventually hurled itself into the loch near the hotel.

A golden eagle soared overhead for a bit, and then flew down and sat on a boulder – a good distance away from Carol, of course. She was excited to think she'd seen a golden eagle and felt quite sorry when it decided to fly off between the peaks and out of sight. She knew there must be other creatures up here, too, but they'd have seen her, of course, and so remained hidden.

But nothing up here apart from the eagle moved at all – there was not even a rowan tree. Funny, Carol thought, the feeling that came over you in this great silence. No movement. No sound save that of the burn. You felt you could cut this huge silence with a knife – that it was something solid. And she could well imagine here that there was no one else in the world but herself –

Suddenly she was brought sharply back to earth. Furious yowling and spitting and dog-yelping was coming from a corrie some distance away, and seconds later both dogs came leaping out of it over the stones and heather towards Carol who, concerned, was standing up and calling the dogs frantically, so that they'd come running in the right direction in their obvious panic. But although Trigger came bounding along, Rex was gradually slowing down, as though hurt.

Then she saw what all the noise was about.

They were being closely followed by a fully grown, very large wildcat – and, the Clachanites would tell you, there is no fiercer wild animal in the British Isles today. . . .

Carol was petrified. She had never seen a wildcat before even in a zoo, but nobody could mistake what this was – like an outsize tabby cat, but looking a hundred times fiercer, and although Trigger was well in front and seemingly unscathed, it was obvious that Rex had already been attacked, because he was running with difficulty. And the cat had almost caught up with him.

Just then a shot cracked out, echoing from summit to summit all around the glen. Carol, who had started to go towards the oncoming dogs, regardless of the fact that she'd been told that wildcats were said to attack man unprovoked, and unmindful too that she had nothing with which to defend either herself or the dogs, stopped dead in her tracks and glanced round in the direction whence the shot had come. She saw a young man fording the burn, his gun held high above his head to avoid its getting splashed. Automatically, she waved a hand, then ran on towards Rex, now lying on the ground exhausted. The body of the cat was stretched out nearby where it had fallen when the young man's shot had killed it instantly.

Because of his injuries, Rex seemed unable to get to his feet. He was whining softly, the long gashes in his sides and back bleeding profusely, and he wanted Carol to know how awful he felt. There was a gash in his head too, and the girl, miserable at the dog's plight, tried to staunch the bleeding of the wound with her handkerchief, which was totally inept for the job. She tried to ascertain if his eyes were damaged, and decided that the vicious claws had just missed them. She was kneeling beside the dog and speaking reassuringly to him when his rescuer, dripping with water from the burn, ran up and he too knelt on the ground beside the injured animal. Carol's relief at seeing him was even greater than she would have admitted to herself, and what was better, Rex seemed to know this young man and was trying feebly to wag his tail. The man, tall, dark-haired and clean-shaven, wore a kilt.

'Hullo!' he greeted. 'I had just come through the gap in the hills over there when I saw what was happening. As a matter of fact, I had come here after wildcat. Several pairs live in the rocky corries around here, and they're becoming too numerous – a perfect menace, in fact. My father's place is through the gap there, and each night the cats come through and kill our people's poultry. By the way,' he said as an afterthought, 'my name's Diarmid.'

Carol nodded, telling him her name, and he bent to examine Rex's injuries, giving as his verdict that the dog would have to have quite a lot of stitches put in.

'Well, we'll get him home as soon as we can,' he finished.

'But – how?'

'I'll carry him.'

Carol told him that shooting dead on target as he'd done, just one shot being enough to kill a running animal, was nothing short of a miracle. But he pooh-poohed the idea.

'I just had to take the risk,' he said, 'praying I wouldn't hit the dog. The cat was coming along facing me, so one shot *ought* to have been enough to kill it – and thank goodness it was.' He took one of Rex's paws in his hand. 'Poor old boy!' he said kindly. 'We'll get you home soon.' He stood up. Carol stayed down by Rex a minute or two longer before she too stood up.

'Would you think there was a wildcat in the corrie that clawed Rex,' she queried, 'because this big one never actually caught up with him, did it?'

'Yes,' Diarmid answered. 'I would think so. I'd think that the dogs found the female and the kittens in the corrie, and the old man heard the rumpus and came running just as the dogs were leaving as fast as they could go.'

'Are we just going to leave the body here?' Carol asked.

'No. I'll take it down to your uncle as he wanted a wildcat skin for a friend, I know,' said Diarmid, and, taking his handkerchief from his soaking jacket pocket, he proceeded to tear it into three, and these three pieces he knotted, to make a longish strip. 'Could I borrow yours too?' he asked Carol. 'I won't tear it.'

'It's covered with Rex's blood – '

'Never mind. It'll make this sling a little longer. What I'm doing,' he went on, 'is trying to make a sling to carry the cat's corpse down to Craig House.'

'But how?'

'Like so,' he replied, tying the cat's forepaws together with one end of the sling and its hindpaws together with the other end. Then he took off his coat, slung the cat across his shoulders, handed Carol the gun to carry, wrapped Rex in his jacket so as to hurt him less, and set off towards Craig House. Carol sincerely wished she hadn't come so far, as it meant scrambling over the rough ground for a good long way even before reaching the path, which Aunt Annabel had told her not to leave. They tried to carry on a desultory sort of conversation, but it wasn't easy to do as they clambered along ledges and scrambled over the heather and rush-clumps, and round great boulders. Eventually they saw Craig House in the distance, though still a good walk away. Carol, grateful to Diarmid for helping her out of what might have turned out to be a truly terrible predicament, thought him a pleasant young man, and certainly good-looking, with his dark wavy hair and long-lashed brown eyes, and she decided he had a good-humoured mouth too. 'And thank goodness,' she thought, 'he's clean-shaven!' She detested beards, especially if they were unruly ones, like her uncle's and Kenny Mor's!

It happened that I had to go into Rhinn that morning to buy socks for my plough, which would soon be in use now. The 'share', by the way, is what in the north is called the 'sock'. There was one shop at Rhinn, and it belonged to Angus-the-Shop. Here one could buy all sorts of things for crofting and fishing without going right over to the other side of Scotland for them, to Inverness or Dingwall, for instance.

I called in at Craig House to see if Carol would care to come with me for the drive. Aunt Annabel told me that Carol had gone for a walk in the mountains with the dogs, so I said I'd leave Myrtle there and go and meet her.

That was how I came to meet up with Carol and Diarmid and Trigger, and the injured Rex. Trigger dashed up to me, and when we all met up I thought Diarmid looked as though he'd been carrying the fully grown Labrador, Rex, for a long, long time, for he looked decidedly tired. And, of course, the cat's corpse wouldn't have been a lot lighter! The ground must have been awful to negotiate with a couple of weighty bodies to carry around at the same time, and when they told me where the encounter with the cat took place, I knew they'd be feeling glad they were in sight of Craig House, though still about one and a half miles away. I insisted upon relieving Diarmid of the cat, slinging it around my own shoulders – which I must say I didn't like doing all that much, but this was one of those times when one couldn't bother about what one liked doing and what one didn't.

Once we'd reached the drive Carol hurried on to find the Laird, who met us before we'd reached the house. In places like Craig and Clachan you had to be your own vet as far as possible, seeing you had to bring a real vet out from Inverness otherwise, and the Laird had, in his younger days, taken a course on veterinary surgery. Rex was laid on a sheet-covered table, given a 'whiff' by Diarmid, and the Laird got on with the stitching up, for there was quite a lot to do. Aunt Annabel had brought dressings, and Carol and I kept going with bowls of warm water, and in a remarkably short time Rex was laid in the warm parlour, where Aunt Annabel would watch over him.

Now the Laird insisted upon Diarmid having a hot bath and changing into some of his clothes, while Diarmid's own soaking garments and blood-stained coat could be dealt with by the staff at Craig House. We all had lunch together, and then Carol

and I set off for Rhinn in Myrtle, while Diarmid walked down
to the hotel to see John.

Carol enthused over the scenery as we went along, although
part of the trip must have been pretty worrying to one unused
to roads such as we had then in those parts. It was, unfortunately, imperative that we should take the Craig–Fasach road,
for there was no other way of reaching Rhinn except by boat,
and we ran inland through various passes in the hills until we
came to Fasach Corner, where the road was more level and in
better condition.

The first twelve miles of the Craig–Fasach road was Hell to
all car owners up here. For one thing it was always covered
with loose stones and bits of rock – some big. Although one
side dropped from the unbanked roadway almost perpen-
dicularly for hundreds of feet to a raging torrent below, on the
other side, where the mountains reached just as steeply up-
wards, the stones and rocks became detached from the main
mass by the elements and consequently rattled down and
cluttered the narrow roadway which hugged the sides of this
range.

The only thing to do was to stop the car and get out, and
kick the biggest stones over the precipice where, there being
no habitation for miles and miles, and it was too steep and
grassless even for sheep, the stones would roll harmlessly down
to the torrent crashing over boulders – a long, long way below.

The other trouble dreaded by us all on this road was the
thought of getting punctures on the worst bit, which in those
non-radial-tyre days did quite frequently happen. We all
carried at least one spare wheel up here, and two or more
inners. The only thing to do then was to stop and blow some
air into the tyre if possible, repeating the operation again and
again until one came to a safer place to jack up the car. This
time, though, we were lucky: we only had one puncture

before we reached the Corner, after which the road was distinctly better surfaced, and we hoped for the same luck on the return trip.

But after the rain or thawing snows we had another hazard to cope with on this road before we came to the Fasach Corner. The burns, in spate at these times, would career down across the roadway, the culverts underneath it being unable to take all the excess water. And round a bend we came right on to a good-sized burn.

Carol proved to be an excellent companion. She didn't gasp, scream, lose her head or panic, or in fact do anything to convey to me that she felt sick with fright inside because we might be swept over the edge by the torrent of water Myrtle would have to plunge through. She simply sat tight and said nothing as the little car ploughed steadily on to the other side without mishap.

'For Heaven's sake – ' cried Carol then, suddenly finding she could breathe normally again, 'I just hate to think we've got to negotiate that lot again when we come back!'

'But Myrtle'll bring us through it OK,' I said, trying to kid myself into believing that she would, but I'd experienced this same type of hazard many times before, and, I must admit, I felt every bit as glad to reach the farther side of the cataract as Carol was!

'Have we any more of these "bothers" before we come to Fasach?' she asked a trifle anxiously.

'Well, we won't know until we come to them, I'm afraid, Carol,' I grinned. 'But the culverts do take the ordinary amount of burn water all right – '

'But suppose we just daren't risk it? Where can we turn to go back?'

'There aren't many places on this road,' I replied. 'We'd just have to reverse to the nearest. The sides of the road along this part are too boggy to run on to, I'm afraid.'

She nodded. 'I noticed that,' she said, 'but still – it may never happen, so – '

'So don't let's worry about that hazard until we come to it – eh, Carol?' She agreed with a smile and said no more about it, but I could see she wasn't really enjoying the trip very much!

Then we came to the sharp descent and subsequent steep hill a mile or so from Fasach Corner, after which one's only bother would be likely to be the inevitable puncture, if we struck a bad piece of road before we got to Rhinn – but certainly just along this bit we seldom did, thank Heaven.

Wildcat

4

Angus-the-Shop's emporium

At Rhinn we parked the car beside Angus-the-Shop's emporium and went in, and I introduced Carol, who thought how much his height – over six feet – must help Angus in getting things down from high shelves. She was thrilled with the place. She'd only seen grand shops and huge department stores in Bournemouth, where her school was, so she'd never seen a village shop that sold everything from gumboots to bacon, and from fishing and crofting things to venison and reels of cotton and paraffin, and also some of the essentials for the housewife like meal, flour, sugar and tea.

Angus-the-Shop had been enterprising and this had had its reward, and was appreciated by customers from far and wide, coming by boat, cycle, car, or just shanks's. Carol nosed around in complete bliss while Angus and I were dealing with the plough-socks.

Now in his fifties, Angus had always fancied opening a shop of this kind, and had been saving for it for years and years. Getting the stock together had been difficult, firstly because he wasn't 'in the money', and secondly because he had to run his parents' croft as his father was crippled with arthritis. Eventually, though, his widowed sister came to live at home again, and he was able to leave the two women to run the place in the summer when most of the heavy work had been done, take a job in Inverness, save as much money as he could, and return home in time for the harvesting. By the end of his first summer he had enough to buy two derelict cottages, and he used the stones to build a longish building, and had it thatched at first. Later he was able to buy some corrugated iron sheets second-hand from one of the crofters to roof the place more smartly for the type of shop he wanted.

The next money he earned went towards his first 'stock . Weaving tweed, for which he built himself a loom, brought him in some more money from the markets, and he again took a job in Inverness for three months in the third summer. With this he bought more stock, and he was finally ready to start in a small way on the project that was so near to his heart. Angus-the-Shop was known now all over the place as a 'supplier of just what you wanted in an emergency', too, and for some years now he had stocked oilskins and other clothing useful to the people of these crofting and fishing communities, besides all the other general stock he kept in good supply.

'Well, even if I'm far, far away,' laughed Carol as we drove back towards Craig, 'I'll always be able to remember that wonderful smell of paraffin and oilskins and cheese and bacon and tarred rope, all mixed up into one gorgeous odour, quite pleasant, too, but so different!'

Obediently, Carol had invested in a pair of gumboots and an oilskin coat and sou'wester, for these were essentials up here, and Aunt Annabel had wished her to buy them.

We had also had other bits of business to do with Angus. Kirsty sent in several dozen eggs, and Beth a lot of skeins of hand-spun knitting wool for the heavy socks the men wore with their stout leather boots. Angus paid for these items cash down. Then Aunt Annabel wanted some reels of cotton, Kirsty wanted some baking tins, and Fearchar wanted some fine sandpaper and a tin of varnish.

Carol and I wondered if travelling the thirty-six miles home without a puncture was too much to hope for, and it was. We only had two spots of bother, though, and both were punctures! One we had a spare wheel for; the other needed a spare 'inner', and that took longer, though with Carol lending a hand it was a quicker job than when I got the punctures on my own. She also got out and kicked all the bigger stones over the edge as she had done coming.

We eventually arrived back at Craig House about six o'clock. Diarmid, once more arrayed in his kilt, was coming down the drive on his way home. We met him as we were driving towards the house. I asked him if he was coming to the *ceilidh* Kirsty was throwing one evening next week so that everyone might meet Carol.

'Oh ay,' he grinned. 'I'd no' be missing a *ceilidh* of Kirsty's! It always amazes me too how Fearchar can remember all the tales and legends and things that he does! Have you ever been to a *ceilidh*, Carol?' he asked her.

'No, never,' answered the girl. 'I'd never heard the word either until I came up here.'

'Och, you'll enjoy it,' he told her. 'We all enjoy ourselves there.' We said good-bye then, and, with a parting wave of the hand, Diarmid cut off into the mountains to take what he was pleased to call his 'short cut': we reckoned even then it would take him a good hour to get home, for after he had walked through our Laird's lands, he had to go through his father's lands beyond the nearest mountain range before he came in sight of the house.

The next afternoon was the first time the Laird could spare to walk down to the hotel with Carol. She was introduced to Fiona and John, not forgetting Blister, John's almost human boxer dog. Catriona, the local schoolteacher, came in while we were having tea and joined us at the table. She had brought along some things made by a crofting family up the lochside for the hotel's shop which would be reopening soon for the season.

The shop adjoined the hotel garage, and sold knitted and hand-woven goods made by the crofters from all around the lochside, and always included a few of Fearchar's professional-looking shepherds' crooks. The hotel guests and passing motorists bought these things, and the sale of their goods meant a little pin-money, which came in useful for all sorts of things that the crofters' wives wanted.

Carol, tremendously interested in this idea, gladly accepted Catriona's invitation to visit the shop, and the Laird and Fiona and John were left to have a little chat on their own.

Catriona, aged twenty-five, was of an enterprising turn of mind, and it was largely through her efforts that the little shop had got going the year before. Once Catriona had organized it, the crofters' wives took turns to mind the shop and sell the goods. The break from the crofting work for a day now and then was something the women had never known before, so what with that and the fact that they could keep all the money their goods fetched, excepting for one penny out of each shilling, made the shop very popular. The penny in each shilling helped to pay for the petrol used in fetching them and taking them home, and in paying a little towards the food the hotel sent in to whoever was on duty.

Carol and Catriona eventually got talking about another project Catriona had in mind – that of somehow raising the funds to provide the lochside people with a village hall. Carol was most enthusiastic, saying that she had all the time in the world on her hands, with nothing to do – and she wasn't a person who *liked* having nothing to do!

'So I'll be delighted to help you in this project, Catriona, in whatever way you wish,' she finished.

Finally, before they went back to join the others, Carol

promised her new friend that she would tackle her uncle about Catriona's idea, and ask him if he'd be prepared to lend the money for the purchase of timber for the building of the place until she and Catriona could pay back the money within an appointed time. And who'd take on the building of the place?

'Well, the local men, I'd think,' replied Catriona. 'They built the hotel shop for nothing for us, saying it was in a good cause, so possibly they'd think this was in a good cause too.'

'We'd best go in and join the others now, hadn't we?' she added. 'But let's not say anything about the village hall proposition yet – '

Carol agreed. 'No,' she said. 'Let's wait until I've seen Uncle....' They went into the staff sitting room, to burst in on what was to Carol a most interesting conversation. Tea was finished, and the friends were all sitting around the room in easy chairs, smoking and discussing the news topic that must now be in current circulation, as news spread quickly via 'Highland telegraph', helped a good deal by Fearchar.

About an hour before, Fearchar had come in all excited and worried with the news that Hannah MacRae, a cheery robust girl of seventeen from the lochside had set off on the previous afternoon to walk through the mountains to stay for a few days with some relatives who were crofting tenants on the lands of Diarmid's father, and she had apparently not arrived there. Jean-Post-Office at Clachan had received a phone call from the girl's relatives and had asked Fearchar to take the message along to the girl's mother, as she couldn't leave the post office. Hannah had had to go past a deep dark lochan where the water-horse – a big black stallion – lived. It was said that like all the water-horses, or kelpies, this beautiful beast could change its form into a very personable young man, lure a passing woman to walk and talk with him, then suddenly change back into his water-horse form and gallop off with her to his lochan, never to be seen again – the sad ending of so many Highland tales.

'But if the water-horse hadn't got her, where could she be?' asked Fearchar, when Fiona looked a bit doubtful.

'Water-horse?' queried Carol. 'Do people still believe in such things?' The question was offered to the room in general when Fearchar had gone home.

'Up here they do,' Catriona replied, 'and no doubt still do in a lot of other places where "modernization" hasn't yet struck. And fairies too. I did until I went to live in Glasgow while I was training. Belief in the supernatural's still very present in remote places, where if the relative or friend of the missing person thinks he or she has been kidnapped by either the Good People or the water-horse, it's not much good thinking they'll ever see them again.'

All this was, of course, quite new to Carol.

'And so they think that the water-horse has got Hannah?' she asked.

'Yes,' said John, 'but the Laird and I are waiting for an hour to see if they bring Hannah in. If not – '

'We'll go, and we'll walk along a little farther,' the Laird added. 'Hannah might have some reason for not wishing to go through the Gap. You never know. She may have gone on to the next pass – '

'Well, she'd still come out on the Laird of Aros's property,' John put in.

'The Laird of Aros? Is he Diarmid's father?' asked Carol, remembering that Rex's rescuer had said he'd come through 'the Gap'.

'Ay, Carol,' the Laird answered. 'Iain MacDuff, the Laird of Aros, who owns the lands next to my own here. A nice chap – and so's his son. Diarmid and Dugald pretty well grew up together. Aros's property is on the farther side of the range on your left as you go out of Craig House drive, and the two passes through are one at the Gap and another about a mile farther on.'

'Well, I hope the girl's all right,' remarked Fiona.

'Och, I'm sure she'll be all right,' grinned the Laird, 'so long as she hasn't strayed from the rather indefinite path, and she's not likely to have. These Highland girls know their way around in the mountains, and they don't take chances. Still, she may have gone on – '

'I never thought before about the mountains belonging to people!' Carol said. 'Can you just go in and out of anybody's lands as you want to then, up here?' She sounded astonished at the thought.

John burst out laughing. 'Of course! There's no law of trespass here so long as you don't do any damage to the property concerned,' John explained.

'And I'll bet you never thought you'd learn about so many strange things in one day, did you?' asked Catriona.

Carol agreed that indeed she hadn't, adding to her uncle:

'Well, Uncle, will you be remaining here for a while with Fiona, John and Catriona? I promised I'd stay with Rex for a bit to let Aunt Annabel go for a walk, so I'd better go home now, I think. Thank you both for a lovely friendly time.' She smiled, and Fiona told her to come down to have a cuppa with her and John whenever she wished. And homewards she wended her way, lost in her thoughts, for these things she'd heard today had brought it home to her how far she was now from the modern life she'd been used to.

A short time after Carol had left the hotel two climbers turned up asking for accommodation for the night, and also saying that they had a message for them from a girl they'd met in the mountains named Hannah. The Laird asked them if they'd come through from the main road that went from east to west, several miles farther on than the Gap, and they said yes, they had, and they'd met the girl nearer to the main road than to the Gap.

'She asked us if we would kindly get a message to her people for her. She was quite all right and had decided not to go to her relatives after all, but to walk on to the main road, and get a lift into Inverness where she intended getting a job. She would write to her parents, giving her address in Inverness as soon as she was settled in a job.'

One of the young men went on to say that Hannah had told them she'd wanted to go and live in a town for a long time, and now she'd seized the opportunity, since her parents would have expected her to stay always and work on the croft. Catriona's lodging was in a croft-house near where Hannah's parents lived, so she offered to take along the message at once, and waving good-bye, she drove away.

'I expect, like Fearchar, they'll be thinking the water-horse has got her, don't you?' Fiona asked the Laird.

'Ay,' he said, puffing out smoke from his pipe, and taking the pipe from his mouth, went on: 'I'm afraid, like Fearchar, they'll be putting her disappearance down to that. . . .'

Corran   Sickle

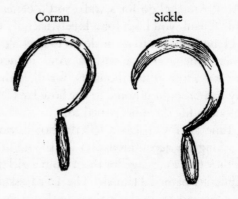

5

Planning the village hall

A couple of days later Carol turned up at my croft-house. I was down the croft building up some of the old walls that the animals had knocked down in the winter, when the crofts were thrown open to the sheep, wild goats, deer, Highland cattle and horses that were wintering out. The croft gates were opened after harvest was in, so that the animals could come lower down, away from the drifts in the mountains higher up when the snows came. The hay would be in the barns, for as Fearchar remarked, 'If it was stacked here, it would be eaten in a short time, and growing crops for our own livestock's hard work enough, without supplying the whole north-west.' So all the crops except potatoes and turnips, which were clamped, were housed in the barns, of which most of us had two.

Because the sheep, goats and deer leapt everything, and seldom used the open gateways like the cattle and horses, we consequently had this annual pantomime of mending the old drystone walls, or renewing fences if we were rich enough to possess any. The repairing all had to be done before the spring-work, that panic of all panics, could start. It would, as a matter of fact, start the very day that Beth sped around the place declaring that she'd licked her finger and held it up in the air, and the cold coming on one side of it indicated that the east wind was with us. It was then we could start on all the work outside, and would go on at a furious rate all through the summer. The east wind would blow for three weeks, and in this time a year's supply of peats – about 30,000 – could be cut by each crofter, and would be dry enough to stack.

At this time, too, we were rushing hither and thither up and down the croft cultivating the land, ploughing, harrowing, planting and sowing – and making meals and mashes for the young livestock, and doing the hundred and one other things that go to make up a crofter's life. Anyway, from the time the east wind arrived for its stay of three weeks until harvest was in, life was one long mad panic.

So I was busy building up some of the old walls, the trio spread out around me in various attitudes of repose, when Carol came bursting with news down the croft to find me.

'I biked along,' she said, 'to give you the latest news – about my uncle's reaction to the idea of the village hall scheme.'

'That was good of you, Carol. I'm dying to hear it. Is it good?'

'Rather! Wonderful, I'd say – '

'Well, let's sit down on this pile of stones for a few minutes while you tell me about it,' I said. 'I'll be coming up to the house soon to make a cuppa – ' So I sat down, and after hesitating a fraction of a second, Carol did the same. Of course, the clothes we wore on our crofts couldn't be more awful, but who'd put on their better garments for the jobs we had to do? Carol was beginning to get more used to us and what must have seemed strange carryings on, but the clothes she wore weren't, of course, of the type that would stand immersion in the burn on washing day accompanied by a good stamping-on with the feet! Her clothes would require dry cleaning, and the nearest dry cleaner's would be at Inverness or Dingwall, both eighty-plus miles from Clachan. Hence her quick glance at the state of the top stones on the heap, to see if her very nice suit would get dirty. But the stones had had a fair amount of rain beating down on them as well as snow recently, and were therefore washed clean. So the peewits' storm had been of some use!

'And now for your news – '

'It's simply *super*!' she blurted out in her boarding school jargon. 'I had a long talk with my aunt and uncle about Catriona's proposition,' she hurried on, 'and they both think it's a smashing idea! Uncle asked if we had any idea yet what we were going to do about building a hall. I had to tell him "no", of course. "We'd need to get funds first," I said, "to buy the timber for constructing it. And then there'll be chairs and things to get before we can ask people to come." Then I asked them if they could suggest any way for us to get enough money for starting off the project. And I added that we wouldn't have to pay builders' costs for putting the place up, because Catriona thinks the local men would put it up in their spare time, like they did the hotel shop.'

'And did either of them come up with any suggestions?' I asked.

'Did they *not*! Just listen to this, Miss Armstrong. My uncle said that the big double boathouse about a mile from Craig had been empty since Dugald, my cousin, went to America, and it wouldn't be wanted again, so he'd give it to us. He thought it would make a fine hall when it had been altered a bit inside and redecorated – and he went on to say that it was in very good condition. Was I sure that the local men would do the alterations – just like that – for nothing? I said yes, and it would be marvellous to have the hall just waiting for us! 'Catriona'll just about burst with excitement!' I told him – '

'Well, I'm thrilled, too, Carol,' I said, 'and yes, I'll bet Catriona will be. That's saved you both a bit of fund-raising, hasn't it?'

'Yes, but you haven't heard it all yet! My aunt said she'd give

us twenty-five pounds towards the fittings – chairs and things –
and my uncle said he'd pay for all the new timber we'd need
to get for altering the place, *and* we hadn't to think of paying
the money back to him because he feels it's all in a very good
cause. So there we are – we'll be able to get started on the hall
right away, and it should be ready by the autumn, shouldn't
it?'

'That's wonderful!' I said, getting up. 'I'm not going on
with this wall any more just now – I'm too excited! Let's go
up and have a cuppa. And Catriona hasn't heard the wonderful
news yet?'

'No, it's only just happened.' Carol stood up. 'But I'm going
to walk along to the post office when school's likely to be out,
and I'll phone Catriona from there to the school before she
leaves for home. I'm dying to hear what she'll say! We were
getting a little depressed whenever we thought how much
we'd have to raise before we could get the thing started.' We
began to walk to the house, and Carol asked if I'd heard the
latest about Hannah – the girl from the lochside who disappeared a day or two ago. I hadn't.

'Well, two climbers brought a message to the hotel from
her. She met them. And Hannah's not so silly either! Apparently she'd been wanting to get a job in a town for some time,
so she seized this opportunity. She intended getting a lift into
Dingwall or Inverness when she reached the main road, and
told the men to say she would write home as soon as she got
settled in a job. The men apparently told Fiona that they
thought she'd have no difficulty in getting a lift all the way, for
there's quite a bit of traffic along that road – it leads to the
coast – '

'A long walk for her, wasn't it? The road's through another
range of mountains,' I remarked.

'But, according to John, from where the climbers met her
at the beginning of a long wide glen, with some greenery in it

as it descended gradually towards the road, there was a little
path which would take her right through the mountain range.
It wouldn't take her all that long, either, the men said.'

As we arrived at the house and were just entering the kitchen
we caught a glimpse of Beth coming out of her gate and turn-
ing in this direction.

'Beth'll be coming here,' I said, 'and I don't think it would
do to say anything about what's happened about the hall, until
Catriona herself fires off the starting gun, do you?' And Carol
agreed.

Beth came into the kitchen, and the trio, having followed
Carol and me indoors, selected their resting places and went
off to sleep. Beth had with her, as usual, her long wooden
knitting needles, and on her back was the creel which always
caddied her big ball of homespun wool, which she used to
throw into it while she knitted herself along the track. As she
greeted us she sat down on the stool she often took if she was
in a hurry, so that she wouldn't have to unhitch her creel.

'Ach well,' she began as she adjusted the wad of straw she
wore wedged into the waist-band of her skirt to hold the knob
of one of her needles; for that was the way most of them knitted
up here – and like lightning, too!

'Myself'll be for gathering a few creels of seaweed for the
tattie ground, whateffer,' she said, 'and I was for wondering if
yourself'd be coming down to the shore to get some for
yourself?'

'No, I'm sorry, Beth,' I said, 'I can't spare the time today.
I must do that soon, I know; but perhaps I'll be able to go down
there for a couple of hours tomorrow.'

'Ach well, then. Gather the seaweed I must,' she smiled,
'because if the east wind starts blowing – any day now – I'll
have no time, for it'll be peat-digging time then.'

'Why? Why do you have to wait until the east wind blows
for anything?' Carol asked, looking puzzled.

'Because then there'll be no rain for three weeks – the east wind being a drying one – and we always dig our peats then because they dry so well, you understand?'

'Oh, I see,' Carol answered. 'And does everyone dig peats?'

'Well, everyone used to, Carol,' I answered her quickly, because it was always a sore point with Beth that I had turned over to coal. 'But some of us use coal now,' I went on. 'We can get it delivered by the truckload – and the man who delivers it shies it down in a black mountain right outside the gate!'

Beth giggled. ''Deed, that's so!' she murmured.

'But can't everyone get coal here if they want to?' the girl persisted.

'Ach well,' answered Beth, 'you see, the peat's free. The coal costs more than some of us can afford, and has to be brought from Inverness. That's if we want it. But myself, for one, would always prefer to burn peat, even though it means so many walks up the brae and so much hard work when we're up there.' She got up. 'If you're no' coming down,' she said to me, 'myself'll be going – '

'Have a cup of tea with us first, Beth,' I begged, but she said no, she'd better not stop. And off she went.

'I like Beth,' Carol said to me when we saw through the window that Beth had almost reached the gate. 'But does she always wear black?'

'Always,' I replied, handing her a plate of home-made biscuits. 'Life's been very hard for Beth, I'd think,' I added.

'And she knits her black woollen stockings herself?'

'Yes, and knits the thick socks in that homespun wool that you and I took over to Angus-the-Shop's to be sold. Angus buys the socks she knits by the "dozen pairs" bundle.'

'I shouldn't think she ever wastes a minute!' remarked Carol. 'And she's dreadfully thin. Her legs are so thin that her stockings twist around them like corkscrews – '

'She is thin,' I agreed, 'but I think she works off any fat – I mean, she eats good meals, so it's not that she's on a slimming diet or anything. If she were to put on any weight, she'd never rest long enough to keep it on! She and Seumas lavish everything they can on old Mairi, Seumas's mother, who lives with them. They're simply wonderful to the old lady but, I must say, she does what she can in return, though she can't do a great deal, seeing as she's only two years off her century! Beth makes all Mairi's clothes as well as her own, and Seumas's shirts, too – and all by hand! I've repeatedly offered her my machine, but she prefers to go on doing things by hand.'

'How does she get the material? There aren't any shops here.'

'Well, she gets material from the mail order firm we all patronize. In fact, that's the way we buy things we want if they're items we know we can't get from Angus-the-Shop's emporium. He doesn't sell material by the yard, anyway.'

'I'd think that that mail order firm is just the cat's whiskers to people living in out-of-the-way places like these,' remarked Carol. 'But for the sake of all the crofters' wives around here, I'd say that a shop nearby would be the best solution.'

'Indeed it would,' I agreed. 'With public transport nil, there isn't the time, apart from the question of money, to go on any shopping sprees to the towns over on the east coast.'

'Well, I do hope that Beth will be able to spare the time to come to the hall sometimes when it's opened. The breakaway might do her good, if nothing else.'

'I quite agree.'

'Well, I think I'll go along to Jean's now and get her to put me through to Catriona at the school – '

'And ask her,' I called as she opened the door to go out, 'if she'd care to come straight here after school. It might be more convenient for you both to chat this business over privately – I'll be down the croft anyway, so you'll have it to yourselves.'

'All right,' nodded Carol. 'I'd think that's a fine idea – and I'm sure Catriona will, too. Oh, I'm bursting to hear what she'll say when I tell her the news!' And off she went.

Beth came in again not long afterwards. She'd evidently miscalculated the tide times. Actually, none of us could see the shore itself from our croft-houses, as it was a long way down, sloping steeply all the way until it levelled out at the bottoms of our crofts, and as there was a bank above the shore, we couldn't see the nearer rocks nor the tide-line unless we were down near the foot of the croft. So Beth had chanced it, and what a pity! Because after going right down to the shore she'd only managed to gather seaweed for a few minutes before the sea had come in too high for her to get on with the job, and then she'd had to drag herself all that way up again. Anyway, a cup of tea cheered her up before she had to rush off to get her cows in off the brae to be milked.

Work was Beth's whole life. The weekly pay of a chauffeur-handiman at that time was not all that good, and they had Mairi to keep on Seumas's money, too. Beth therefore made what she could on the side; any produce she could spare went to Angus-the-Shop, and the mobile shop bought eggs, milk, butter and cheese from her whenever she had an opportunity of selling the produce to them. Which unfortunately wasn't often because she had to wait until someone was going over to Angus's, and the mobile shop only came along the track when it suited Duncan Van to brave the potholes.

Mairi was a hale and hearty old lady for her age, and she liked gardening as much as baking, so she made herself useful to Beth and Seumas doing both these things. But up here the soil wasn't good enough to grow vegetables well, so we all banked in a square of the ground near the back of our houses with big stones from the brae and filled it with the best soil we could find, to a height of about eighteen inches. Things grew well in it – better, Mairi said, in spite of the attention they got, than those Beth insisted upon growing in the front garden as extras. Old Mairi was always doing something in the back vegetable garden, keeping it watered and hoeing the weeds out, etc., but it meant she had to go up the three steps – three big stones from the brae – to reach the soil and plants, and of course there was nothing to hold on to. This concerned Beth and Seumas very much, but they couldn't think of a solution to the problem.

Carol had not been back in my house more than a quarter of an hour when Catriona drove up, looking very pleased at the girl's news, and after I'd made them tea and put scones and biscuits on the table I left them to have their talk. I had to get the cows in for milking anyway, and I stayed out and did the milking too before going in again. They were still happily planning things when I returned to the kitchen. Finally, when they did depart it was almost dusk, and Catriona wouldn't hear of Carol biking home, for it would be dark before she got there.

'The track'll be dangerous to bike along in this light,' said Catriona, 'and the sheep'll be all over the road by now, all the way to Craig. They seem to prefer the stony surface to the heather – but don't let anything surprise you up here! But you might have a nasty accident if you ran into one of them round a bend in the road. I'll put the bike in the boot.' And Carol gratefully accepted a lift back to Craig House.

6

Maniac on the roads

Early the next morning I was up with the lark's song. I wanted to finish the wall repairs, collect seaweed from the shore for the potato ground, make butter and turn the cheeses, and have a look at the chitted potatoes in a shed. And I had come to the end of the scones in one of the tins, so I'd have to find time to make some this morning somehow, before anyone was likely to turn up. And in the afternoon I'd promised to take Peigi MacLennan out for a driving lesson. It all sounds a lot to cram into one day, although there was more to it than that, actually – the usual chores added on: meals and mashes for the young livestock, milking and buckets of water to carry in from the burn. But it was actually quite an ordinary day's work for a crofter, and somehow, when you weren't chivied around and could fit things in yourself as and when you pleased, it never seemed a hardship, and it all got done without a fuss.

Peigi, a very punctual person, arrived on time.

'For ages,' she told me as we got into Myrtle, 'I've been watching what people did with the gears and things when they were driving, and I'm believing that I know pretty well what to do.'

'Well, even if you do think you know, Peigi,' I answered, 'there's a terrible lot of practice to get in before you're safe to

go on one of these roads on your own, I'm afraid. You've
never actually driven a car, have you?'

'Ach no. But, you see, we're having Willie Gunn's car – it's
paid for and he's bringing it tomorrow. Himself's bought a
new one. Indeed, it's I who'll be driving him home again,
whateffer, so I *must* learn all the essentials today.'

'Peigi, you can't rush things like that!' I cried.

'Ach well. I'm thinkin' that I'll have to. I know a good bit
what to do – '

'Let me see you run through the gears,' I said, 'before we
start.' She did this and, much to my surprise, she knew which
was which – and the gearhandle wasn't marked either. A short
time later, after three or four tries with the gears, and some
attempts at starting and stopping and reversing, we started off
along the track, and I must admit she went along carefully
then, avoiding most of the potholes quite well. But when we
reached the end of the track, where it joined the road to Craig,
she must have decided she knew everything there was to know,
and began tearing along at a rate far too fast for that wicked
switchback road beside the loch.

'Slow down, Peigi, for pity's sake!' I begged her, gritting
my teeth, and clinging on to the seat for all I was worth.

'Why? We're all right – ' she shouted back, reducing her
speed not one whit. I closed my eyes, wondering if she remembered how to stop if she had to.

But there was no attempt at stopping or even slowing down,
and on and on we rushed, and all I could do was hope we
wouldn't meet anything coming towards us until she'd made
up her mind to cut her speed down, or until we came to a hill
steep enough – which would be as soon as we passed Craig –
for the engine to do it for her. I'd almost got to the stage of
grabbing the wheel from her hands; but that would probably have meant we'd go over the edge and down into the
loch, to sink without trace.

We dashed past Craig Hotel, on past the drive to Craig House, and on up the awful Craig–Fasach road – the one Carol and I went along a few days earlier. And suffice it to say that I thanked Heaven for that stony bit where we had to get out and kick the bigger stones over the edge. She *had* to stop then, and I tore her off a strip about not only endangering her life and mine, but that of the other road-users if we met anything. 'Speeding like a maniac'll get you nowhere!' I fumed, getting out to kick the stones over. She had managed to stop, put the gear into neutral, and pull the brake on firmly – all of which surprised me. She must have noticed quite a lot about other people's driving. . . .

Fortunately, one met very little on this road, for which I was grateful to its appalling condition, for a change. We'd have been for it before this, had there been some traffic.

Having got over the stony bit without a puncture, Peigi now speeded up again – and how we ever reached the Fasach Corner intact I shall never know.

Having endured what I had done coming here, it was purgatory to think we'd got to do it all again going back – but worse, because there was more 'downhill' going back. I was terrified Peigi would take the corners on two wheels – and gave up hope of ever seeing Clachan again!

Of course, we got a puncture – and who, in these days of pneumatic tyres, wouldn't have done? But we swopped the punctured tyre for the spare in no time and were quickly on the road again.

That was, all in all, one of the most frightening drives it's ever been my lot to experience, though Peigi thought it was all lovely – tearing along with her hairpins lost and her hair streaming in the wind when it wasn't across her eyes, which didn't seem to trouble her in the least. We did, however, have one little happening which I should report before I close this episode, thankfully. That was when, coming up the lochside road on the way home, Peigi spotted Fearchar coming towards us on his bike. She took her hand off the wheel to wave to him and shout. The result was that Myrtle took things into her own hands and ran on to the squelchy verge – on the other side of the road to the loch, fortunately – and Fearchar, gazing after her in surprise, saw what happened and came back to help push the little car on the road again, much amused. Peigi thought it very funny too, apparently, and it didn't shake her at all. I wondered if she was ever frightened about anything! But I was beyond smiling then.

'I'm glad you're both amused!' I said acidly, and thanked Fearchar for coming to our aid, and then Peigi resumed her faster-than-sound progress towards the beginning of the track when, thank Heaven, she had to slow down a bit to avoid the potholes. . . .

Peigi only came out driving that one day, and I don't think she had any other beginner's drives at all. She just managed herself. But how she got off for quite a long time without having an accident will forever remain a mystery to us all! And then one day the inevitable happened, as it's bound to do with someone who knows it all. She was going so fast along the lochside road that coming to a blind corner she couldn't brake or change gear in time, and she charged round the corner into a wall! The car looked like a concertina; Peigi was lucky for, apart from a few bruises and one or two small cuts from broken glass, she herself suffered little more than mild shock. The car, however, was a complete write-off, but it was covered by insurance, so she did in time have another car. But everyone noticed that she drove at a far more reasonable speed after her spot of bother, which must have saved some of us from joining our forefathers before we'd finished our allotted life-span.

Beth came out quite a lot with me, in Myrtle at first and later in the brake, and Seumas took her out in the brake for a practice whenever he could now, too, if I was too busy. She was a careful and steady driver, and was all ready to start driving on her own when Seumas bought his first car a few months later. Seumas drove for the Laird and had always wanted a car of his own, and Beth had sent everything she could to Carol's stall, and to the hotel shop if it was knits she wanted to sell, to get some money to go towards the car. They had their new car just before the hall was opened, so Beth could manage to squash in the time between tearing about to do this or that to put in an appearance at the hall, even if it were only for a short time; also the lifts she was able to give her neighbours were much appreciated. Petrol was the big worry, and the Rhinn pumps were private ones, Gregor and me being allowed to have ours from there as a concession.

So, seeing it would be so useful now, John had a pump put in at the hotel – but one always had to allow for twelve miles before one ran out, and this was remedied by Gregor's bright idea to sell petrol cans, which he bought in bulk and sold at almost cost price to all friends and neighbours who needed one – and this saved the situation on many occasions.

One afternoon I was milking Geal when Jean-Post-Office turned up to give me a message from Catriona. It appeared that the minister had told her he wholeheartedly approved of the idea of having a village hall, and that he fully appreciated that there'd be a lot of expenses to be incurred before the hall could begin to function. He would be pleased to help in any way he could, and it had occurred to him that as chairs would be one of the big expenses, the proposed hall was so near the church that if it would help, once the hall was open, the organizers could borrow the chairs from the church for the time being, provided they were taken back to the church after the meetings.

'Well, thank you for bringing along Catriona's message,
C

Jean,' I said, 'but this thing's not my pigeon. It's entirely on Carol and Catriona to deal with it; still, I'm delighted to hear that the minister's backing them up, all the same – '

We had just got to this point in the conversation when Geal, very touchy about being disturbed when she was being milked, kicked out with her hind leg and had me, milking stool and bucket all over into the drain. I picked myself up, and Jean, horrified and full of apologies, hurried off back to the post office. I took self and accessories along to the burn, and we all had a wash; but you can't stop milking a cow in the middle of proceedings, so back I went to continue with the good work, and Geal, as though contrite about what she'd done, couldn't have stood more still and peacefully cud-chewing for the rest of the operation.

But the drain in the cowbyre wasn't the most salubrious place to wallow in; so when I'd finished Geal and milked Bess too I stood the buckets in the dairy and hurried to the house and put on everything in the way of a container for water I could spare on the stove. When it was hot enough, I poured the water into the zinc bath I'd brought in and stood by the fire.

Now, if I'd got myself terribly dirty anytime working on the croft and didn't want to wait until the evening before I had a bath, I heated water and hurriedly had a bath between doing various jobs – and it was as though people were drawn to my house by a magnet. Somebody always came at that time, although I mightn't have had anybody for two days if I were presentable. Today was no exception. Fearchar arrived a few minutes after I'd got started, to put my name on a rota for borrowing two horses for ploughing from those of our community who had them.

I always took the precaution on these bathing occasions of wedging the latch on the kitchen door, and of putting a heavy armchair against it too, barring entry. Now I called through

the sponge that he couldn't come in as I was having a bath. If
he wished to wait until I'd finished I wouldn't be long; but
having been kicked sidelong into the cowbyre drain by Geal –
and not for the first time – it had been very necessary for me
to have a bath now instead of this evening.

He agreed that I'd need the bath, told me what he had come
about, and said he'd wait in the hall – there was a chair there,
thank you – and he could discuss my place on the rota quite
well through the door. Now he automatically raised his voice,
although with Fearchar there was no need to, for his ordinary
voice would, I'm sure, be heard over at Ros.

Twenty minutes later, washed, changed and in my right
mind again, I opened the door on to a pea-souper of Black
Twist. His pipe must as usual have been doing yeoman service.
Now accompanied by the fog, he walked into the kitchen and
sat down. I left the bathful of water until later, because it meant
ladling it all out with an old saucepan and throwing it outside;
instead I made a cup of tea.

'Myrtle took no harm from her run on to the verge yesterday, did she?' he asked as we drank. He had a very soft spot for
Myrtle.

'None,' I replied, 'thanks to your coming back to help push
her on to the road again. I think if she'd had to stay there until
something had come along she'd have sunk lower, and
maybe over her exhaust, which wouldn't have helped things
really.'

He puffed a few clouds more, then he said, 'Well, well. You
were no' long, yourself and Peigi, getting to Fasach and back,
whateffer –'

'No. I should think it must have been one of the fastest runs
for that trip!' I declared. 'I'm only just coming out of my
coma, and I'd rather not be reminded of it. Let's talk of something else. Have you got everyone on your rota now for the
horses – re the ploughing of the various potato grounds?'

'Oh ay. I'm believin' ourselves are all on it now.' He proceeded to count down the list to where my name would come.
'Yourself – well, there's a space following Kirsty's. Would
that be all right for you? It's rather soon; but yourself'd rather
have the horses then, would you no'? Or would you prefer
later – after Kenny – '

'Soon, thanks, Fearchar. I'd rather follow Kirsty, if you
don't mind.'

'Ay – well yourself'll be fifth on the list then – Rory Creels,
then Moira (the deaf and dumb gorl), then Anna, then Kirsty,
then yourself – leaving a day between each for the horses to
rest up. Each is a hard day for them. . . .'

'Of course. Shall I give you the money now for the hire of
the horses, Fearchar?'

'No, no. Later'll be best, mistress. Meanwhile, should you be
going to Angus-the-Shop's for anything for the spring-work,
there's several of ourselves'll be needin' things for you to bring
back.'

'Well, let me have the list as soon as you can, will you? I'm
not sure when I can spare the time to go, but – in a day or two,
yes, all right.'

'Fine! Myself'll bring you the list – '

'By the way, are you going to dig peats this year,
Fearchar?'

'Och, well, I'm thinkin' myself'll chust finish out the peats
I have left, then go on to coal, whateffer,' he grinned. 'It's all
my life I've dug them, but I'm seein' coal can be delivered to
Clachan if one makes arrangements – '

'Well, if you know when they're bringing it, it would be
OK I suppose, but you must have seen the arrival of mine –
when I was down the croft. That great black mountain – right
outside my gate! Still, it's a lot better for me than spending all
that time I haven't got to spare up on the brae, digging in that
black boggy mud – '

'Ach – I'm feelin' I canna be bothered now – '

'And about a week from now, Fearchar,' I laughed, 'no-body'll feel like sparing the time to dig peats! – unless, perhaps, Beth. We'll all be wishing the days were twice as long anyway!'

Cotton-grass

7

Winkles — and news of the electrics

The mobile shop had braved the potholey track on one of its rare visits to Clachan, and Duncan Van had kept his longstanding promise to bring me several crates which I could make into hen-coops. Several hatchings were due out, and I was in a panic, working against time to have the coops ready, when Carol blew in, having come along on Moira's bike.

'I've only got a few minutes,' she said, 'but I just slipped in to tell you I had a lovely time at Kirsty's yesterday. We were sorry Jean couldn't come, and the talk started about the awful hours she had to do on that job. Everyone thought that Sunday for her day off was about the worst day they could have thought of, as she can never go out even for a walk with these elders of the Kirk so against it, and she's never been able to get anywhere, shopping or anything, since she came. I think it's simply *awful*!'

'Yes, we all do, Carol, but Jean's against anyone making a row about it for her, because she says she knew she'd only have Sundays when she took the job over.'

'Well, I'm going to speak to Uncle about it – but I won't tell Jean I'm going to – '

'Don't for Heaven's sake make any trouble, Carol,' I said. 'Wouldn't you think it would be as well to see Jean about that first?'

'No, I'd rather not get her involved. I'll have a chat to Uncle about it, and we'll see what happens.'

'And you met all the younger element here – at Kirsty's?' I asked her.

'Oh, yes. It was so nice of them all to come to meet me, and I enjoyed being at Kirsty's so much. How are you getting on with the hen-coops?'

'Oh, all right – but I guess I hammer my thumb as often as I do a nail!'

'Never mind. It's all in a good cause!' she laughed. 'Well, I hadn't better stay now,' she said, 'or I won't get back before all the sheep are lying all over the road – '

'No, Carol. Don't risk that,' I said. 'You'll be along again in a day or two?'

'I will. Until then – good-bye for now. . . .'

I saw her off at the gate, and I thought, 'There goes a person who'll get things done. She really does get on with a thing – not just talk about it. . . . But I only hope they won't take offence up here. After all, she's only been here such a very short time. But I'll bet she won't wait until tomorrow to have her chat with the Laird about Jean's off-duty day!'

The upshot of it was that I saw the Laird and Aunt Annabel stop the Daimler outside Kirsty's two days later. Carol was determined to nag her uncle into doing something about Jean. Only *he* could deal with the authorities about Jean's off-duty time, and she got down to giving him the gist of the whole thing that same evening she had talked to me, with the result that he rang up and explained the situation to the authorities who hadn't realized that Jean was never off-duty excepting on Sunday, when she couldn't shop nor visit friends. If she was to leave, the Laird pointed out, it would be exceedingly difficult to fill the post again, because no young person would be likely to want to come to such a remote place and never get out of it for a break, etc. It worked, because eventually they said that if Jean would train one of the local people whom she could trust absolutely to take on from her sometimes, so that the post office was never left unattended on a week-day, she could take a different day off. And the Laird had come up to tell her about it himself.

Jean, who had no idea that anything was afoot, was extremely surprised when the Laird, having dropped Aunt Annabel at Kirsty's, walked along to the post office with the news. Jean was very pleased.

'And I think,' said the Laird, 'that it would be a good thing if you would be so kind as to keep to yourself the fact that Carol was instrumental, really, in getting this thing sorted out. She herself was very conscious that some of the people might think she was poking her nose into things that were no concern of hers instead of minding her own business.' And of course Jean agreed to comply with his wishes. She was delighted that now not only would she and I be able to go off for drives in Myrtle and have picnic meals somewhere in some beautiful spot, but now she would be able to have a real shopping spree in Inverness occasionally.

Aunt Annabel had seized the opportunity of having a lift to Clachan with her brother, as she was dying for a chat with Kirsty over 'a wee strupach', for they had been friends for many years. And over the wee strupach they thrashed out the affairs of Clachan, and the county council, and the prices of things, and thoroughly enjoyed themselves.

'And what do you think of the village hall idea, Kirsty?' Aunt Annabel wanted to know.

Kirsty took her time swallowing a mouthful of jammed scone before replying, a bit hesitantly: 'Ach, well. Catriona's been keen on the idea for a long time, you know, but she didna get the backing. However, now herself has Carol – so keen on the idea, and a young lady who is as ingenious as herself, and liking to have something to do all the time, the pair of them together'll no doubt get somewhere in the matter of a village hall.'

'But you're not so pleased about the idea, Kirsty?'

'Well, now. I canna say that. It *would* be a good idea, but nobody up here is used to having any spare time! When the day's work is done, it's off to bed they are, because they're all up early in the morning – and, of course, for quite a lot of the year it's hardly dark at all during the night, so themselves'll be working very late – often, as yourself well knows, until after midnight on the croft. And then there's the transport bother. There isna any, so how in the world would any of us get to this hall?'

'They've thought of that,' answered Aunt Annabel. 'Everyone with cars has promised to join in, and so a shuttle service will fetch people and bring them home.'

'Is that so? Indeed, it's very good of the car owners – '

'And the girls are hoping to get started by the time harvest's in,' said Aunt Annabel. 'You know, Kirsty, I'm sure you'll enjoy it as much as any of them, when you've been down to one of the meetings there. There'll always be tea and scones and things, and people will be able to chat with those whom they never have a chance to otherwise. And Catriona's going to hold various kinds of classes that'll be bound to interest some people, like sewing and embroidery, making rugs, making leather gloves, making things for the house – oh – all kinds of things'll be made, and if they don't want them when they've made these things, they can be sold in the hotel shop. Catriona learnt to make a lot of these things in her training, of course, and Carol has had certain lessons at school for making useful things for the house, she says, so they'll take the classes at the start. Later, they may be able to afford to get people to take advanced classes. And there'll be dancing, and as soon as Carol's mother's affairs are settled, she says she's going to buy a gramophone, so that there can be music in the hall sometimes – and for the dancing.'

'My! But those girls *are* going to work hard!'

'They are, Kirsty. And that's not all. Carol's going to buy a movie camera – '

'What in the world's that?'

'Well, she'll be able to take photos of people moving about, walking and doing all sorts of things. And the people in the hall will be able to see themselves on film – on a screen which they can put up on one of the walls; but you'll see them all actually moving.'

'Ach well. Myself'll like to see these moving people, whateffer.'

'That's good, Kirsty. Oh, here's my brother coming up the path – '

'And I'll chust be getting a wee strupach – ' and, disappearing into the scullery, she came back almost at once with a small tray containing the same items as his sister's tray had on it.

'Jean'll be very pleased at the news, whateffer?' Kirsty asked as she gave the Laird his tray. 'I'm sure!'

'I think she was,' he replied. 'Overjoyed, in fact! D'you know she's never had a chance to do any shopping – '

'This was what's been so sad,' said Kirsty. 'When Bella-Post-Office had the place, she didna want to shop – nor ever to go out of the village, in fact. And yet now herself's living in Edinburgh – a married woman! But because she never minded about going to Inverness for some shopping, I suppose that nobody thought anybody else would until now, when yourself's got better times fixed up for Jean. As things are, though, I'm telling you, if Jean was to leave, there's nobody would ever take this post office again. Young people'd no' be coming here to the job, whateffer, because they like being in or near towns nowadays.'

'That's what I told the authorities,' the Laird said.

'I was telling Kirsty about Carol being promised a movie camera,' said Aunt Annabel, 'and Kirsty's – '

'Ach, well. I'm finding myself looking forward to seeing pictures of people moving about – on a screen,' Kirsty chuckled. 'None of us here have ever been to see the "movies" as you call them – '

'So it'll be a new thing for you all, and you'll be able to see them down at the hall as soon as it's opened,' grinned the Laird. 'I'm sure you'll enjoy the movies, Kirsty.'

'Ay – I expect I will, whateffer. But I chust don't know how ourselves are going to find the time to go – '

'Och – you will, you know,' he laughed, 'and Annabel and I will be coming to share in the pleasures, too.'

'You will so?'

'Rather!' he promised, getting up to go home, and Annabel following. Both the old ladies told each other how nice it was to see each other again, and how they'd enjoyed the chat, and the Laird promised to bring his sister along again soon.

The whole village would have seen the Laird's car. I did, too, and I decided to wait until it departed before I ran across to Kirsty's with the winkles I'd brought her for her tea when gathering seaweed in the afternoon. We all liked them very much. The winkles you got here on our microscopic bit of shore below the croft were very plentiful, and, to my mind at least, extremely nice to eat with thin bread and butter, or, failing yeast bread, thinly cut soda bread. The winkles clung to the underside of the tangle on the shore, and as that seaweed was often washed up in great masses, you could always be sure of getting lots of them. But they didn't look like the winkles I'd seen anywhere else, small and with round, blue-black shells. These up here were much larger, and their shells were more like those of the whelk though smaller and smoother, and more pale brown in colour than an ordinary whelk-shell. The real whelk-shells here, incidentally, were enormous, and were formerly used for lighting the croft-house kitchens as an alternative to little heaps of guish slivers, one each side of the hearth. When a whelk-shell was used as a lamp it was filled with oil – whale-oil, usually, in those days – and a bit of twisted wool served as a wick.

Anna often used to run down to the shore and gather winkles for Kirsty's tea, but now that she had two crofts to run, Gregor being away all day, she very seldom had the time. So anybody who was going down to gather seaweed brought some winkles up for Kirsty. Now she put them on to a dish from the scullery and came into the kitchen, where we sat in armchairs each side of the fireplace, discussing spring-work, which everyone would be panicking about the next day.

'Beth's gone up to dig peats already,' said Kirsty, 'and it was only this morning that she rushed round to us all saying the east wind was blowing. She gets really excited about digging the peats. I wonder why? Until recently when I've bought coal, I've always looked upon peat-digging as something that's got to be done, not something I'd get excited about doing! She must have had everything ready to have been able to start off digging right away, but the others'll all be up there tomorrow. The potato planting'll start next week.'

I said, 'Yes, Fearchar had put me down on the list – fifth, I think – so it will be the following week or the one after, for me.' Then Kirsty told me what the Laird had come up about, and how Jean was so delighted. 'And Aunt Annabel and I had a nice long chat. Ourselves feel very much the same about lots of things, whateffer,' she said. 'And she seems to get on all right with Carol. I was afraid there might be trouble there, because one's so modern and the other's no modern at all.'

'Well, I think Carol's a girl who's far happier doing something all the time,' I said, 'and that would please Aunt Annabel much more than if she liked to sit about all the time!' I said.

'I'm hoping she enjoyed it here – to tea with the younger people who live around –'

'Oh yes, she did. She told me so, ' I said.

At that moment the door opened and in hurried Fearchar, Kenny Mor and Lachlan, seemingly very perturbed about something.

Kirsty, surprised, looked up as they came in, but Fearchar began without preamble: 'Ourselves have chust been hearing that the electrics are coming to Clachan, Kirsty –'

'Ach no!' Kirsty cried. 'And now ourselves'll have those nasty great pylons – chust ruining the look of our mountains!'

'The joiner has a power-drill now to help him make the coffins and things,' put in Kenny Mor, 'and –'

'And Mairi and Roddy Lochside have a fine refrigerator,' squeaked Lachlan. 'Themselves can keep their food nice and cool in the warm weather, Mairi was for saying –'

'And who'd want to buy a refrigerator chust for the warm weather up here?' asked Kirsty indignantly. 'More like you'd want something to keep your food warm instead of cool, whateffer!'

'Ach well,' Fearchar said, feeling like giving up. 'Beth's come round to wanting the electrics now, after what Seumas has been telling her about how useful they are at Craig –'

'*Has* she now!' cried Kirsty. 'Well, however useful themselves are finding them, it's myself'd chust hate to have to look at a big great pylon down on my croft yonder! Ach – I chust feel I couldna face such a thing.'

'But the pylons down at Craig are behind the hotel, and those along the lochside are well up on the brae – nowhere near the houses, whateffer!' Fearchar explained. This, he suddenly realized, had impressed Kirsty.

'Not where the people'll have to look at them all the time –

and now I come to think of it, they *are* up the brae some distance. . . . But themselves are dreadful-looking things in any case!'

'Well, I'm thinking they'd run them in a row along at the back, Kirsty,' Fearchar pointed out, 'and that'd be no' throubling yourself, would it? It'd only be on the heather.'

'Ach well. No,' said Kirsty, 'I'm thinking if it's *got* to come, the pylons'll no' be so bad at the back of the brae, away from the houses. We have no doors at the back, so we'll no' be having to see them, and the wee window in the scullery can be curtained – '

'Well, themselves'll be starting to dig the holes in a week's time,' said Fearchar.

'Holes? What for have they to dig holes?' Kirsty asked, surprised.

'Ach well, we dinna rightly know,' said Kenny who, with Lachlan, had sat down on the seize – the big wooden bench that was in every croft-house kitchen, and under which the crofters' dogs knew by instinct that they'd have to stay quietly until their masters were ready to come home. 'Ach, theirig! But there must be some reason, whateffer – '

'Ay, and the reason for those holes behind the hotel,' Fearchar informed, 'were for the big pylon they've put up there.'

'And there were some explosions, whateffer, were there no'?' reminded Kirsty. I was taking no part in the discussion. After all, it was their business. I didn't mind lamps and gadgets, but of course, when I'd had electricity in the south, it really was a great help. Still, I played safe from annoying anyone and said nothing.

'Ay, it was because of yon gelatine themselves were using for to make them.'

'I'm remembering seeing some holes – ' recollected Kirsty. 'And I'm wondering whose crofting lands up here will they be exploding with gelatine?' she sighed. 'And it'll no' be my own without a fight, I'm tellin' you!'

'Well, I'm still thinking the pylons'll be at the back,' said Fearchar reassuringly. 'I'm no thinkin' they'll come on to the crofting lands with their explosions at all, whateffer.'

'And I'd hope not,' said Kirsty flatly.

'And dinna forget, Kirsty,' squeaked Lachlan, 'you'll have no need to bother with heating a brick in the fire to put into your iron once the electrics come here. Yourself'll have an electric iron.'

'Ay, and an electric kettle. No more stirrin' the fire to get the kettle to boil quickly – '

'And no more searching for the matches. Chust a wee switchie,' grinned Fearchar, knowing they'd won Kirsty over, 'up on the wall beside the door, and you've a fine light that comes on – whoosh! – chust like that, and you can see where you're going, like in the daytime.'

This chat seemed as though it was likely to go on for ever, so I got up and said I must be going, and the three men also stood up.

'Well, good-bye, Kirsty,' they mumbled, and, 'Good-bye, Kirsty,' said I. At the gate Kenny and Lachlan went on their way, while Fearchar walked with me to my gate and had a few words with me before we went our separate ways.

'I'm thinkin' we've got Kirsty to see that it's no good trying to fight the "electrics" people,' he said. 'We can do nothing about it with them even if we do object to switches.'

'No, we can't, Fearchar,' I answered. 'I'm hearing, though, that Donald and Flora along the lochside have got masses of switches put in – '

'Ach well, well!' he laughed out loud. 'Ourselves have been telling Donald himself'll have to sell a lot of his stuff to pay for them, whateffer – but he's no' carin'. I'm wonderin' if himself's had his bill in yet?'

At that moment Carol walked up the path and joined us. 'I've been waiting for you indoors,' she told me. 'I didn't know where you were, but I thought you wouldn't be long, and I wanted a chat with you before I cycled home again.'

'I'm very pleased to see you, Carol,' I said. 'We've been to Kirsty's. She's not very keen on electricity coming to Clachan.'

'Oh, is it coming along here?'

'Ay,' Fearchar answered. 'Ourselves have been trying to persuade her that it'll be easier for her to switch on the light, rather than hunt for matches in the dark.'

'I'd say it was!' Carol grinned. 'What's the objection?'

'Kirsty wasn't sure where they'd put the pylons,' I said, 'and naturally she doesn't want one looking her in the face from the croft.'

'Ach – they'll be putting the things out on the brae at the back,' Fearchar said. 'Kirsty has no need to look out of the tiny scullery window unless she had a mind to,' he went on, 'but it's no' only the pylons that's upsetting her whateffer. She's too old now to alter her ways, she thinks – so herself told me one day – and the old Tilley lamp that herself's used for so many years now will be hard to discard in favour of something so modern as the electrics, whateffer. And you were saying that Donald and Flora had had a number of switches put in?' he added as he turned to me.

'Well, that's what I heard. And when I've passed their house at night, it's ablaze with light!'

'Ay, Donald thinks it'll help his sister Flora, for she canna see over-well now. There's a switch in the hall, on the up-stairs landing, in the kitchen, dining room and sitting room, and in each bedroom, and he even had one put in the closet, as he said he thought it would be nice for Flora.'

Carol's expression registered surprise. 'That was very nice of him,' she muttered.

Then Fearchar said he must be on his way as he had two

young calves to feed with mashes. Carol and I waved good-bye to Fearchar, and he went down the track to his house while Carol and I went indoors.

'The Clachanites are a bit free with their talk about closets and things, aren't they?' she grinned.

'Free?' I said; then it dawned on me. 'Oh, but, Carol,' I hastened to explain, 'he doesn't mean water-closet! A closet up here is a cupboard or a small room – like those which lead out of the kitchen in most of our houses – where you keep the pots and pans, and if you have a calor-gas stove, it's usually kept in there too.'

'I see,' Carol nodded. 'But speaking of closets, I like the poem that you have framed in the hall – for visitors – '

'Oh, I had some friends – a couple – staying with me last year, and the husband wrote it.'

'Well, please can I copy it down? Jolly good directions, I'd say it gives! And if you'll be kind enough to read it out, I could write it down more quickly.'

I agreed, and she sat down at the table with pen and paper, while I read out:

Visitors please note:
If the loo you do desire
You will find it in the byre.*
Out of front door, second right,
And don't forget to take a light
From the table in the hall, if darkness has begun to fall.

If you think you'd like a bath
You take it by the kitchen hearth,
And with zinc bath you have to cope.
(Please ask for bath-towel clean, and soap.)
In other room the family go
If please, you'll tell them, so they know?

* This was the original byre, not used since the newer one was built.

If hot water you desire,
It's in large saucepan, on the fire.
Sing hey! A crofter's life for me!
No hot-and-cold; no WC!

'Thanks. Well, I've got that all down,' she said, dotting the 'i's and crossing the 't's'.

'Have you got any news – about the hall, Carol?'

'Yes. Catriona met Seumas and the joiner at the boathouse after school, yesterday. I went too. They were deciding how the place was to be altered inside, and what new timber they'd need to get. Catriona asked me if I agreed about what the men suggested. And I said yes, the men are going to put in all the spare time they can on building it – free. It's very good of them, isn't it? But Seumas reminded me that the spring-work'll have started, so we mustn't expect the men to have too much spare time just at present, although he was sure they'll give all the time they *could* spare.'

'And did the men think the hall would be ready for opening just after the harvest's in?' I wanted to know.

'Yes. They said it would be ready by then – '

'That's fine, then. Catriona's very satisfied, is she?' I asked.

'Oh, yes,' said Carol, 'I should just think she is! As happy as a child who's been given a new toy!' She took a drink of tea. 'About the electricity – you're pleased yourself about its coming along the track to Clachan now, aren't you?'

'Rather!' I said. 'How lovely not to have to look for matches or a paper to use as a spill, to bring a light over from the kitchen mantelpiece from the little lamp in the glass paste-pot.'

'And you'll be able to have a kettle and an iron – and a fridge – '

'It'll be just marvellous to have these things!' I exclaimed excitedly.

'To change the subject now,' Carol said, 'I'm going to Inverness tomorrow.'

8

Animal visitors

'You're going to Inverness – how? That's always the question here – unless somebody's going to take you – '

'They are. My uncle's taking me in. He's got a meeting there, and as soon as it's over we're going to look at some cars. I hope I'll see one I fancy, now that I can buy one for myself.'

'And you'll be doing some shopping while the Laird's at his meeting, will you?'

'Yes,' she replied, hesitating. Then she decided she'd tell me. 'I'm also going to look at some movie cameras. I think it might please the people around if they can see things as well as people, moving – on a screen, in the hall.'

'A wonderful idea,' I said.

'And I've got something else at the back of my mind to get down to after the hall's got well started. But please just keep it to yourself. I wouldn't want anyone to know about it but you and Jean at present.'

'I promise,' I said.

'The people here could do with a shop that sells the things – crofting and fishing things, and groceries, too – that they often sorely need. It's all very well getting people to bring you things back from Rhinn, but it's better to buy them yourself, and be able to choose them yourself, too, of course. So I'm planning to start a shop – somewhere that's handy for everyone – perhaps along the lochside.'

'That's a wonderful idea, Carol! I'm sure they'll all be very glad here to have a shop handy for them.'

I suddenly had a thought. 'Duncan Van might take exception to a shop starting up here,' I pointed out.

'Well,' she grinned, 'I'm thinking Duncan Van can just take exception to the idea if he likes! He only has himself to thank. Just look how people are put out, waiting week after week for something. He only comes when it suits himself – so do we need to worry about Duncan Van?'

'Won't it cost a lot to start it off?' I wondered.

'I'll have enough money to start it off. . . . But we mustn't breathe a word – '

'I agree with you, Carol. We'll keep it to ourselves until you ring the gong – ' And now pandemonium suddenly started up along the track. 'Whatever's the matter?' Carol cried, running to the window. The trio had heard it too and Tee-tee jumped up and would have rushed outside, but I shut the door in time.

'It's that bull broken out of its field again,' I said. 'It's lucky you haven't met it yet, because it quite often escapes and comes galloping along the track.'

Corrie, barking, jumped on a chair and stood on his hind legs to see better, and Tee-tee made no bones of springing on to the table with ears back and teeth bared, and spitting and yowling as hard as he could, he got his face as near the window as possible. Of course – my gate was open!

'Oh, good Heavens! What a huge beast!' cried Carol, ducking under the table as the bull turned in at my gate. Tee-tee and Corrie made such a row they attracted his attention. I went into the cupboard by the fireplace. Who knew that it wouldn't break the glass and put its head through the window? And that, although the animal couldn't get in, was too near for my liking!

And what with the bull stamping around outside bellowing and Corrie and Tee-tee doing their worst, and now the hens and ducks all obviously, by the noise, scurrying for safety, the row was quite terrific. At least, it would warn people on their crofts or walking along the track, and, knowing from many previous visits of our pet aversion exactly what was happening, they would rush for the nearest cover.

'I've always been afraid you'd meet the bull when you were biking up here, you know, Carol,' I said from my refuge.

'Well, you won't have to worry any more,' she said meaningly, 'because nothing would induce me to risk it on a bike again! In a car, you have got some protection – '

The animal ramped round to the front window again, and we had a fresh fit of panic from Corrie and Tee-tee, and this time the bull bellowed and put his head so near the glass that I really thought it would get that part of him inside the room, even if he couldn't get the rest of himself in. Carol didn't see what was going on from her hidey-hole under the table, but she could imagine it, she said, and, anyway, I was keeping her posted, as she informed me.

'What happens now?' she asked. 'Does somebody come and fetch it?'

'Yes, when Dougal Bull finds it's gone, he'll come after it.'

'And may that be soon!' breathed Carol.

'It's gone out of the gate now,' I went on with my commentary, 'and I only hope Kirsty's gate's shut.'

Carol came out and stood up.

'Let's go upstairs,' I said. 'We can see the whole pantomime from one of the bedroom windows.' And so we did, and very thankful that we were where we were! It missed Kirsty's, so she must have shut her gate, but we were very worried about Jean, in case she was doing anything outside, feeding the hens or milking the cow or anything, for she couldn't run. Neither could Kirsty, but Kirsty didn't stray far from the house and

outbuildings these days, so she'd be able to take cover at once –
and she'd know what the noise indicated anyway.

Presently we saw Dougal tearing along on his bike. He
might have been in a cycle-race, instead of on our potholey
track!

'Oh, well, our noisy visitor will soon be on his way home
now,' I remarked thankfully. 'I hope he hasn't made a mess of
all the gardens he's gone into on his trip! But he's made a
mess of ours, I'm sure, stamping around like that for several
minutes – '

'It seemed like several hours!' said Carol, still feeling shaken.
'Can you give me a lift home, please?'

'Of course,' I said. 'Now let's go down and have a strong cup
of coffee.' And I was thinking that we couldn't do much to
help ourselves, really, if we met the creature when we were in
Myrtle! A canvas hood – even if you had it up when you met
the menace – and mica side-screens weren't much help in the
way of cover, as I'd found to my cost once when I met with a
berserk cow, and on other occasions when I'd met with the Highland cattle herds around here. I managed to get away quickly
in the case of the berserk cow, and the Highland bulls are
usually quiet when they're accompanied by their harem. But,
thank Heavens, it had never been my lot yet to meet up with
this menace of Dougal's!

Downstairs once more we watched from the kitchen window and were delighted to see Dougal, his owner, pushing his
bike with one hand and leading the bull by a rope in the other.
It was quiet now – as though it had never put the wind up
anyone in its life!

I took Carol home in Myrtle, dropped her at Craig House,
and wished her a happy day tomorrow.

Since Fiona and John wanted me to call in when I could, I
went now, on my way home. Our business was quickly dealt

with, for I knew the light would begin to go fairly soon, and I wanted to get back to shut everything up before it did.

The gist of our conversation was on the subject of the hotel brake. Fiona and John wanted to sell it and get a new one. I thought it a good idea, because a lot hangs on whether you can rely on a vehicle to get you to the train, when it goes once in the day and you're over fifty miles away from it. Hotel guests wouldn't want to have to be brought all the way back to try again tomorrow! So I said I could do with something bigger now, and I'd buy it.

I knew I'd never find anything as reliable as Myrtle, and I hated the prospect of parting with her, but I found that with all she had to do now, carrying crofting things galore and often giving lifts to more people than she ought to carry because there was no public transport up here, it was becoming necessary to think about buying something a bit larger. The time had come now – I'd just *have* to part with Myrtle. . . .

Fearchar and Lachlan would be sad, too, at her going. They always very kindly did all the smartening up of the little car, even to painting her, but I couldn't afford both, so letting Myrtle go was the only sensible thing to do if I didn't want springs and things to go through her being overloaded so constantly.

Myrtle was wonderful on petrol, doing almost fifty miles to the gallon, but that day I'd dashed off with Carol and hadn't stopped to see if there was enough in the tank. And there wasn't.

When I'd got about a third of the way along the lochside, and nowhere near any habitation where the crofter would, I was sure, have cycled down to the hotel to bring me some petrol, I ran right out – and there I was, itching to get back to shut my fowls and things up before the wild beasts got them! There was nothing for it but just to wait for something to come along – and nothing much did along this road at this time, for it was no fun getting out constantly and shooing the sheep out of the way.

Fortunately for me, the road-men, some of whom came from Clachan, had been dealing with the frightful Craig-Fasach road that day, so were a bit later than usual. They said they'd give me a tow, and we fastened on the tow-rope. And from that moment they forgot all about Myrtle being tacked on behind!

We swished from one side to the other of that hair-raising lochside road at something faster than the speed of sound, round corners on two wheels, coming back on four again with a bump, and as we neared the atrocious corner where a big rock stuck out into the road, they had to brake suddenly round the bend to avoid a sheep. The rope got twisted around a wheel and they had to stop – and then they saw Myrtle and me. . . . I barely heard their apologies, and though their speed was reduced considerably after that I must confess that I was very glad when the lorry stopped outside my gate, and the tow-rope was taken off Myrtle. I was nearly in a coma then anyway, and it was some minutes before I felt strong enough to get out of the car. When I could think properly again all I could do was to think what I'd missed – wallowing in the loch with the car somewhere in the deep dark bottom of it!

But now I had to hurry, and I made a quick cup of strong black coffee on the primus, swallowed it as soon as I could, and dashed out to shut everything up. When I got back to the kitchen, I sat down for a few minutes at the fireside, the trio arranged in various attitudes of sleep around me, and I began to think about my car problem. I decided I'd done the right thing by saying I'd have the brake. It had been kept in excellent condition, and would certainly be much roomier. But I wasn't going to let just *anybody* have Myrtle. . . .

As it happened Angus-the-Shop had a friend, Simon, called 'Sim', who had been staying with friends in Edinburgh about

six months ago. At a dance there he had met a girl named
Flora. The couple became engaged almost at once, and after
spending about three weeks at home, getting a house and
everything ready for Flora, Sim went back to Edinburgh,
married her and brought her to Rhinn to live. Flora had never
been to this part of Scotland before and didn't take either to the
people or to the place. The people didn't take all that kindly to
Flora either; although they were polite, and some of them asked
her and Sim to meals, Flora always made some excuse not to
go, so Sim couldn't very well go either, and he was in terror
he'd lose all his lifelong friends through her behaviour.

Fortunately, when he got a chance to slip along to the hotel
bar on a Saturday evening, his friends were just the same to
him, well understanding how things were with Flora – which
they all rather deplored, as Sim had always been popular with
everyone. And Sim was grateful, for life at his home was
getting to be one long Hell. Flora was bad-tempered, and was
by way of being superior and snobby to people, and wasn't
the least bit interested in Rhinn – or in Sim now, either.

Now for a long time Sim had one great wish – to be the
owner of a car. He had learnt to drive in the war, and before
the end of it was the private driver for one of the officers of his
regiment. So not only did he have to know how to drive well,
but he had to keep the appearance of the car and its working
parts in tip-top condition. One day, when I'd run over to
Rhinn for some shopping for some of us, I met Sim there,
having a brief chat with his friend, Angus-the-Shop. Highland
telegraph had been busy, and he'd heard that I was thinking of
changing Myrtle for a roomier car, and he then and there asked
me to give him the first option on Myrtle. He had often seen
Myrtle in Rhinn, and liked her, and as Flora held tightly on to
all the money that Sim earned at his engineering work at
Rhinn's only garage, and only allowed him so much to spend
on himself, he thought that with what he hadn't given to

Flora, but which was secretly 'minded' for him by his friend Angus, that he might be able to afford Myrtle. I hated parting with her anyway; but I'd far rather do so to someone like Sim, who would look after her as though she were a piece of very precious porcelain – and would drive her carefully, too, on these frightful roads. So I agreed to give him the option, and said I'd let him know as soon as I had the other car. Then either he could come over for it, or if that would be difficult, I'd bring Myrtle over to Rhinn to him, and perhaps John would come too – in his car – so that I'd have a lift home.

We knew that Sim slipped away somehow most days for a few minutes' chat with his friend, Angus, so I arranged that John should phone Angus, who would pass the message on to Sim.

Now that I was going to have the brake, John phoned Angus with the message for Sim that we'd be over with Myrtle in two days' time, so when Myrtle and his car went in procession to Rhinn, we expected to see Sim somewhere about. John parked outside Angus's, while I parked Myrtle outside Sim's and knocked at the door.

I knocked three times before Flora, very angry-looking, and made up to the nines, opened the door and said, 'Yes?' No smile was forthcoming, and I sensed trouble in the offing and wished I could become transparent, just like that.

'I've brought the little car,' I smiled. And that was the wrong thing to say, for Flora liked *big* cars.

She frowned. 'Oh – *have* you!' she sniffed, standing up very straight.

'Well,' I said, trying to appear pleasant, 'would Sim be around anywhere, that I might speak to him for a few minutes about the car, do you think?'

'Sim's down at the croft,' she said. 'You'd better go and find him.' I said I would, and departed round the outside of the house, hearing the door banged loudly shut behind me. I soon found him and he began to apologize profusely for not being on hand to greet us; Flora, he said, didn't like him wearing a watch while he was working on the croft, for fear he'd bash it, so he hadn't known the time. Evidently they weren't all like old Fearchar up here, who'd worked out the times of day with no help from a watch – he didn't possess one – by taking note of the distance the sun was from one of the nearby summits.

'John's down the road,' I said, 'at Angus's. He asked if you wouldn't mind slipping down there and having a word with him.' Sim said yes, he would like to see John, and handed me the ten pounds for Myrtle, and I in turn handed him the log book.

'I'm more than delighted to own Myrtle,' he grinned, 'and I hope you'll believe me when I say that she'll be properly looked after – '

'Indeed, Sim,' I broke in, 'if I hadn't known that in the first place, I'm afraid I wouldn't have let you have her. But I've seen you drive Angus's car, and I've heard how careful you are of the cars that come into the garage, so it's all right by me. But what does Flora think about your new toy?'

'Ach – ' He gave a bitter little laugh. 'Flora'd sooner I'd bought a Rolls-Royce! But, as I pointed out to her, we're lucky to get a car at all, and especially one that we know's reliable, and we wouldn't want to pay the petrol bills of anything bigger. Perhaps she'll come round. . . .'

And then something struck me like a blow in the face. Of course. It wouldn't be good enough for Flora, and she'd make him get rid of it –

'Sim,' I said seriously. 'I want to ask you to promise me something – will you promise to give me first option on Myrtle, if you have to sell her at any time?'

'You mean – you'd have her – when you have the other one?'

'Yes. I couldn't tax and insure both of them; but there's no reason why she shouldn't be jacked up under a tarpaulin for the time being, just resting in pure idleness for a time. She's worked very hard always, you know. And later on, after some of the potatoes are sold, I could tax her again maybe. But I'd like to feel I had her again, if you hadn't got her. . . .'

And so he promised. And I was right. I was to have Myrtle back sooner than either he or I imagined then!

On the way back John told me he'd taken a frantic dislike to Flora.

'She speaks angrily to Sim all the time – even in front of other people,' he said, 'and the woman must be barmy, putting so much on her face that you'd reckon she'd done her making up with a trowel. Poor old Sim spends hardly anything on himself, and limits himself to just one wee dram on Saturday evenings – the only time he sees his pals – so Angus tells me. Perhaps he could get himself a few things he fancies if Flora didn't spend the earth on these expensive cosmetics, which I understand she sends to Edinburgh for.'

'Oh, well,' I said, 'thank goodness he puts his foot down about Saturday evenings with his friends, even if he mustn't for peace's sake be gone long; and now he has Myrtle, which he seems very pleased about.'

'Well, what's the betting she'll nag him that it's not grand enough, nor big enough? I think you'll be offered your "first option" for buying Myrtle back soon, don't you?' John said.

'I wouldn't wonder at all,' I answered. 'One thing, though – Sim'll look after the little car, and should I ever have Myrtle back – provided it's had no other owner but Sim, I'd be quite certain that it would be returned in the same condition as it was when I took it over to him.' The little car, in spite of her age, had been thoroughly reliable, even though she'd often been called upon to do yeoman service, and as fortunately Fearchar and Lachlan and I all regarded her as something to be looked after properly, for her age she was, in our opinion, absolutely marvellous.

Carol had her new car. She'd been to Clachan to show it to whoever she'd thought would be interested, and even Kirsty liked it! The date of my potato-planting had come up, and Carol stated her intention of coming to help on both Kirsty's croft and mine. It would be quite different to anything she'd ever done in her life before, and since she'd told Jean that the more she saw of crofting the more she wanted to become a crofter herself, Kirsty said the tatties would be a good thing for her to start with.

The date of Kirsty's planting came round and Carol, arrayed in one of Kirsty's old overalls, went down the croft with the others – for anyone in the village came to help other crofters' potato planting for as much of the day as they could – taking with her a bucket borrowed from the stables at Craig House, and a knife that Cook had loaned her. Alastair, who had the day off work, took the horses down to the level ground at the foot of the croft, and harnessed them to the plough a little later. All of us who'd come armed with bucket and knife turned our buckets upside down and sat on them while we worked against time, cutting the tatties into bits, each with an eye in it, and throwing them carefully on to another heap. Another crofter who had taken the day off work arrived with a sack of guano, obtained from the off-shore islands, where there were masses of sea-birds. When we started the planting, he'd take tinsful of the fertilizer from the sack and, following the plough, would sprinkle a little all the way along a furrow. It may be mentioned here that 'bosses' around this part of Scotland were very understanding about their men taking the odd day off in order to get the ploughing and planting done on their crofts, and nothing was said about it so long as the men said beforehand which day they were taking off. It was understood that the three acres or so of land used for potatoes on any croft could be done in a day, and, in fact, I never knew the operation to carry on any longer. Everybody did their stuff, working hard throughout the day, and in the evening, when the planting was finished, whoever's 'planting' it had been would have a fine big tea waiting for the workers when they came in after work.

Carol joined in the cutting with gusto, and then, when Alastair and Seumas were ready to begin the ploughing, she and the other helpers took up their 'beats'. This meant that they stood in a row a number of feet apart, armed with a bucketful of the cut-up bits, and when the plough had finished one furrow and had turned to come up to do the second, the row of helpers, one by one, dashed forward to put in the pieces of potato about eighteen inches apart all the way along the furrow, on top of the guano. The furrow from the next row ploughed would completely cover the potato bits, and so on, until the whole area was planted.

Carol thoroughly enjoyed herself. It was a joy to see the girl entering into the spirit of things like she did, and even in this short time she really wasn't regarded as a stranger any more here.

My planting was to be in two days' time, and she said she would be coming to help then, too – and she did.

The second week in June, and chicks and ducklings, still small but growing well, had hatched out in May, and now the crofters' wives were kept very busy making mashes and feeds. We had to be careful that things flying above didn't swoop down and whisk off our youngest stock. A good cockerel was the best investment, we found, for he always kept a look-out for anything hovering overhead and gave a warning cry; it was quite amusing to see everything – hens, ducks, ducklings and even full-grown ducks – rushing for the nearest cover.

They got very good at it, for in this part of the world they had a good deal of practice!

Our main worry all the year round actually was getting our hands on some wood, perhaps particularly at this time of year, when we needed things like extra hen- or duck-houses and the coops for young poultry clan members. Duncan Van would bring us crates ordered some time before – *when* he came – but our best bet was to collect driftwood from the shore. All sorts of slats and beams and old wooden boxes got lodged in amongst the rocks that lined the loch, and we used to bring what we could of this home and dry it out and use it for countless things about the croft. It was no good trying to wash the salt out of it for it was impregnated through and through, but dried out we could make good use of it.

Lugging it up from the shore was rather a bind, I must admit, but if you live in a place where there are no trees at all except the one inevitable rowan in each front garden to keep the evil spirits away, which, of course, nobody would dream of cutting down, you had to get wood from somewhere, for its uses were legion. With Duncan Van only coming erratically, and the only other way to get wood was to go down to the shore for it, after a stormy sea had been running which would always wash a lot of wood up amongst the rocks, this latter was a much-appreciated source of supply.

However much we dried it out, though, if we used it for the fire, we had to watch it carefully as it sent out thousands of burning little sparkles, each one of which could have caught something on fire.

Once our potato-planting days were past and the turnips in most of our crofts by this time, Kirsty and I had a little spare time to do some of the things we'd been wanting to do for weeks – just until the hoeing started, followed by the annual excitement of who was, and who was not, going to the 'Communions', an annual gathering held a few miles down the

D

coast, and which all who could attended. Those who didn't looked after the animals of those who did. Sheep-shearing started about a week after the Communions people got back, and sheep-dipping followed.

Neither Kirsty nor I were going to the Communions, so we were kept busy from morning until night making and taking round mashes and feeds, cleaning out, milking, etc., for several crofts besides our own. But having each made up our minds that we wanted to put up some more shelves in our sculleries, I went down to the shore one day to find good and strong pieces of wood that would do.

Having collected a number of suitable bits of driftwood, I climbed the bank, deposited an armful at the foot of the croft, and went back for more. While I was climbing the bank with another lot, and having my back to the loch, I suddenly heard a noise like a hard-worked soda-water syphon behind me. I dropped my armful and stood paralysed for a moment. When I dared I turned round – and beheld an enormous whale only a few yards away from me. Our loch was so deep that submarines had trained in it, so I wasn't all that surprised, once I'd come to properly again after my fright, to see a whale spouting merrily only two or three arms' length away from me. This wasn't the first visit he – or at least any whale – had paid to our loch, as Beth had told me once that they came in occasionally, 'and like the mines,' she added, quite disinterestedly, 'he always goes out again with the tide....' I'd only seen him once before, soon after I'd come here to live, and then he was doing just what he was doing now: spouting his way gaily down the loch to put the wind up anyone in a rowing boat – and as Beth said, he just spouted his way out of the loch again with the tide, into the open sea.

The people here were not interested in whales unless they were dead. Gregor used to tow in any he found stranded and dead on any nearby beach, and used to divide it into great chunks so that those in Ros or Clachan could have some to melt down for oil if they wished. So a dead whale was quite something in Clachan and Ros, and so was its smell. It was revolting to walk along our track on the occasions when almost everyone was melting down their pieces in big fish-kettles or iron pots outside, beside the burns. I always thought paraffin smelt awful, but whale's a lot worse!

Carol came over to see me after visiting Kirsty and Jean the day the whale glided down the loch at rather close quarters. She asked me if they'd kill this one for oil or something.

'Not now,' I said. 'They would have years ago, but they're not so dependent upon whale-oil now because they can buy paraffin from the hotel if they take a container.' Myrtle often took a number of containers, because she did most of the to-ing and fro-ing for paraffin for Clachan.

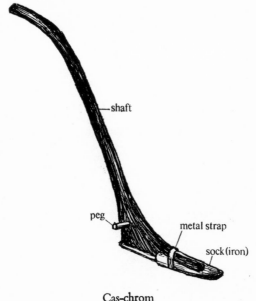

Cas-chrom

9

Carol settles down

Of the incidents which happened frequently, the whale's visit was of course filed into the harmless category, but they weren't all harmless – not by a long chalk. A couple of days after that we had sheep-worrying problems to contend with.

Every crofter had one dog, mostly two, and sometimes one of them suddenly went berserk without any warning and killed sheep. But these dogs were crafty enough to do their killings at night, when nobody was about, and very often another dog, not his *usual* companion, went with him. We couldn't let our dogs out at these times, because the men would shoot on sight any dog seen on the braes. After seeing the havoc that two strange dogs had done this time, we weren't feeling soft-hearted about their demise either. The killings spelt great losses to the crofters and meant that their wives often had ten or more motherless lambs to bottle-feed several times a day.

The day after the killings, Carol accompanied the Laird when he came to sympathize with the Clachan crofters and their wives, and see for himself the extent of the damage. They were both aghast at what they saw, and although Carol shed a few tears at the sight of the dead mums and tiny lambs on the brae, nevertheless she made herself extremely useful, running to help first one person, then another.

Carol was finding her car very handy already, and, because she could get around more quickly, she was becoming very useful to the lochside communities, and, as she never minded in the least what she did to help, very popular too. In no time at all she came to know people on both sides of the loch, and in the isolated, tiny communities on the other side to Clachan and Craig her visits, either by boat or by scrambling round the edges of the mountains, were looked upon with great pleasure by the crofters and their wives over there.

When she came up to Clachan in her new acquisition she confessed to me that now she felt a lot safer when in the vicinity of Sambo, the bull of the Highland herd, or of our bull, which might at any moment break out of his field!

Carol was a very alert, observant sort of person. She didn't miss much, but fortunately, although she often felt that the people wouldn't need to work so hard if they did things another way, or felt that things might be improved in various ways, she had the good sense to keep her thoughts about these things to herself, excepting now and then letting herself go on about what she called 'the lack of ambition' to Jean or me.

We tried to make her realize, though, that most of the people in these parts had worked terribly hard all their lives, and that now they were old, all they wanted was to have just the essential things to do, and since the young people all went off to the towns, and would never come back here to be content with a crofter's existence, it was best to leave them alone. They were quite content with their lot.

Carol still thought they might provide themselves with a few luxuries with no effort to themselves. If they could be persuaded that they could realize money for their surplus produce, she would be prepared to sell these for them.

Jean and I both wondered how she was going to go about it.

'Well, I could have a little stall on the side of the main road,' she replied, 'and now there are more motorists coming out this way for drives, and since many more tourists are coming to the Highlands each year, I don't see that there should be any trouble about selling nice fresh eggs and butter, chickens and perhaps ducks, and surplus potatoes and anything else at the roadside, do you? After all, they've been doing this sort of thing in the south now for years, and those roadside stalls – farm stalls as they call them – do jolly well.'

'I shouldn't wonder,' smiled Jean. 'And if when Carol's sold the produce for them they see how farm stalls can do very well even right out here, I should think it would spur them on to grow more with a view to selling it, wouldn't you?'

'We both think the same, Carol, I'm sure,' I said. 'But have you thought that Aunt Annabel and the Laird might object?'

'I'll have a talk to them about it tonight,' she said confidently. 'If I could just start the ball rolling, so to speak, get them to be enthusiastic about it, I'd think that in a short time we'd be able to get out a rota, because they'd like to sell the stuff themselves!'

'Carol,' Jean said then, 'I think it's a splendid idea, but it'll all have to be handled very carefully, as regards getting them to sell their surplus produce – '

'Why? If they only give their surplus potatoes and things to the animals now, don't you think they'll see the sense in making a little extra money out of selling them instead?'

'Yes, quite, but don't jump it on them, Carol,' I said. 'Talk quietly to Kirsty about it first, I'd advise. See how she takes the idea. If she likes it, she can do the publicizing better than any of we three can, seeing we're new boys in Clachan – '

Carol nodded. 'Yes, you're right, I expect,' she said resignedly. 'They probably wouldn't like to be told things – especially not fresh ideas.'

So it was arranged that Carol would go along to see how Kirsty took it, then sound out the Laird and Aunt Annabel. At the end of all that to-do, if she felt strong enough, as we told her laughingly, then go ahead, and the best of luck!

So it was all arranged: Kirsty and Carol's aunt and uncle seemingly had no objections. Eggs, butter and cheese surplus could be sold right away, and no doubt more and more people would be interested and bring along their stuff for sale soon. Then later this produce and cartons of cream – Carol would get the cartons in Inverness – and potatoes and other surplus crops could be sold as they became available.

A day or two later Carol went into Inverness to buy tarpaulin for the covering of the stall, and as Diarmid had offered to make the framework and fit the stall up for her, he went with her. Together they bought timber, strong thread and sturdy needles to sew the canvas, and trays and other containers for the produce display. They planned to have the stall ready in about a week, and if they started trading, say, on a Saturday, then on Friday Carol would run around with the car to collect the goods for sale from Jean-Post-Office, who had undertaken to collect everything.

Meantime, the hall was going ahead with the alterations, too, and it was pretty certain now that the opening could be arranged for the week preceding the end-of-harvest *ceilidh* at Kirsty's. There was, what with everything Carol had set out to do, a tremendous amount of work. Catriona spent each evening and week-end organizing it all with help from Carol, Diarmid, and Fiona and John when they had a little time to spare. The men who were giving up their spare time in the evenings carried on nobly with the alterations inside the late boathouse, so that already it was taking shape. They were also partitioning off two small rooms, one for the kitchen and the other for anything where a smaller room might be needed, like meetings, lectures, craft classes, etc., at the same time as the bigger hall itself was in use. A grand opening had been planned, and Carol hoped to have plenty of movie film ready by then as an added attraction.

Carol said that if the people gave an indication that they liked the films, she was prepared to hire films – documentaries, plays, etc. She always had her movie camera with her now, so that was how, just at the right moment, she was ready with her camera when there was a little set-to with Sambo and Co. versus Fearchar.

Carol had joined us all that day to help Fearchar get his turnip-dibbing done. He had little time nowadays to work his croft because he was down at the hotel, coping with all the outside work there each day. The last effort in the spring-work was the dibbing-in of the turnip-seeds, planting two seeds in each dibbed hole ('one-for-the-pigeons-and-one-for-the owner'), as they all did up here. And later Carol confided to me that she hadn't known before that birds could count! But it was a hit-and-miss game anyway, because the seeds were too microscopic for anyone to bother counting out two!

Lachlan and Kenny had to go home in the middle of the planting to see to young stock, and they didn't fasten the gate to the track securely. Fearchar hadn't had time to cope with his lazy-beds yet this year, and had intended doing them that night, after the turnip-dibbing. Lazy-beds were resorted to up here when the ground was too rough and/or stony for the plough. Fearchar had brought his sackful of cut-up potatoes down the croft to the lazy-bed ground, emptied the sack and taken the latter on down to one of the barns, meaning to bring some grain for the fowls back in it. He'd taken his cas-chrom down earlier. This method of planting potatoes was very hard work, but it meant that the bad ground was not wasted, and potatoes seem to grow as well on bad ground as good up here!

The cas-chrom was a kind of foot-plough. You pushed the metal end – a kind of plough-sock, or share – into the ground with your foot on a peg near the bottom of the shaft, and you turned a furrow this way, working backwards, until the furrow was as long as you wished it to be. Then you dropped in the cut pieces of potato about eighteen inches apart all the way along, and the next furrow covered them. And so on until all your potato-bits were planted.

Well, Sambo and Co. were coming along the track and, seeing that the gate had blown open a bit, in they all trooped, found Fearchar's potato-pieces, and ate the lot. Carol happened to look up in that direction, and she called out to Fearchar, who, seizing a fencing-stob in lieu of a stick to wave at them, hurried up the croft brae and managed to shoo them back towards the gate and track again. Carol wasn't sure whether Sambo might take umbrage at Fearchar's shoo'ing and waving, nor were we; while we all took cover in a barn, Carol stood on a knoll with her camera and filmed the whole thing. Still, as she admitted later, she had it all worked out that she could have got to the barn in time if it had been necessary. But we knew Carol by now. She'd have gone to Fearchar's aid if she'd seen – as she could from where she stood – that he needed it. However, Fearchar's potatoes were gone, and as all his others were planted he had no spares now, which upset him a bit at first. Later, when Kenny came back and was told what had happened because he and Lachlan had left the gate insecurely fastened, he said he had some left which he would bring along to Fearchar directly the dibbing-in was done. So that little incident ended up less sadly than it might have done.

Carol ran down to the hotel a good bit these days and was always delighted to have something to do, so Fiona and John were delighted to give her jobs – and she never minded what they were. If there wasn't anything to fill in her time in the hotel itself, Fearchar was always willing to oblige, teaching her how to milk the cows, do the dairy work, feed the poultry, and even shear the sheep when the time came round. She was pleased, because at the back of her mind there was always the wish, acquired since she came up here, to be a crofter herself one day.

Diarmid often came to visit his friends, Fiona and John, as he and John were great buddies. The former was good at carpentry and made odd things for the hotel and the new hall, and also made the stall for Carol's farm shop, as well as trays for the display of the croft produce to attract the passing motorists.

Carol went into business as planned, and was completely sold out on her first day. Diarmid stayed all day and helped her, and in the evening they rolled up the stall, for he had made it 'collapsible', and Carol took it back to Craig House. The stuff for sale at first was mostly from Clachan, and there was great excitement when she and Diarmid took the money for the sale of the Clachanites' goods to Jean to distribute when they came in for it later, as arranged.

Fearchar, Seumas and Kenny urged the lochsiders to sell their surplus stuff at Carol's stall. Catriona's landlady collected the produce for the lochside, so the stock was kept up, and people soon began thinking it would be worth while growing more, since Carol could apparently always sell it to the tourists.

Sambo and his harem were rather dreaded by Carol at the stall, but Diarmid was free to go along and help her – which meant driving Sambo and his glamour girls away if they came that way – until the end of September, when the stall closed for the season anyway. He would have less time to spare after that because he was taking MacBean, the factor's, place, caring for his father's estate from the end of the month on. . . .

Very soon the people living in the scattered little communities on both sides of the loch were bringing their produce for Carol to sell at the stall. She had said that she wanted the people to keep the whole of the money she got for their goods, but everyone thought the stall ought to be run on a businesslike basis, and eventually she agreed to deduct a halfpenny in each shilling towards the various expenses she'd incurred – paper bags, boxes, cartons, etc.

Now that the June weather was warmer and more or less settled, and the peats stacked and the crops in and beginning to come up, Kirsty reverted to one of her 'herding' bouts. These interested Carol no end, for herding was something she'd never seen before; it was new to me too until I came here to live, for I'd always thought of it as a thing of the past.

The grass, young now, was good on the crofts – better, Kirsty used to maintain, than that on the braes, where it was so mixed up with heather and all manner of other things. So when it was a nice day she would try to spare a couple of hours to drive the cows down her croft to graze the better stuff – strips of which she had Alastair and Anna leave between the bigger areas of crop grounds. She herself used to take down her knitting with her and sit on a big stone, and here she would knit and sing the old herding songs. Carol took her camera with her one of those days and asked me to come with her, for Kirsty might perhaps object to being filmed. But Kirsty didn't suffer from stage fright but acted her part very well, and in fact it turned out to be a delightful film. However, herding was a fidgety business: you could never reckon to sit down for more than a few minutes at a time because you had to keep on shoo-ing the cows off the crops that were coming up because, if left, they'd very soon graze all your crops too! The cows would keep on doing this sort of thing, and I used to wonder if cows were really as brainless as sheep, as they never seemed to learn to keep on their own strip of grass. Perhaps, though, they were just being deliberately naughty. . . .

10

Sheep-shearing time

It was the end of June – and sheep-shearing was the next item of importance on our agenda. We all took a hand at this job, and the men took their holidays at this time. Shearing by hand, one person could do on an average seven or eight sheep an hour. With the whole of Clachan helping, we reckoned we'd get through the couple of thousand or so sheep in about fourteen or fifteen days.

At first the men only got a week's holiday, but when this Laird took over, he realized that they'd got to get their own croft-work dealt with and cope with their families and animals; provided they arranged it so that they weren't all off together, he didn't mind if they wanted to take their holidays at this time – and he increased the holiday to a fortnight. Seumas was, however, the only man from Clachan who worked on the Laird's estate, so of course there was only one person off for holidays.

At this shearing time, our sheep were driven down, shorn and dipped in a remarkably short time. There's no doubt that the method the Clachanites used to catch sheep was the best. Several of us went up the brae with stack-nets, and these we would throw over the lambs, each one separately. Our Scottish stack-net mustn't be confused with the enormous English one!

Ours were of necessity small because our stacks, if anybody sported a stack up here, were small because of the gales. A big stack would have been blown away or eaten by visiting wildlife almost as soon as it had been built up, so practically everyone put their hay into the barns. But whether we had stacks or not, we all kept a stack-net by for emergencies, and they came in handy quite frequently.

To do the shearing we all used to sit outside, along the verges of the track, because if bits of fleece hung on to heather and rushes, it wasn't as though you had your garden cluttered up with it for weeks: the wind would blow it away if it wasn't collected. As a matter of fact, the odd bits came in handy for lots of things when they were washed, and some people collected them and spun them up and knitted or wove them. Some of the older women washed it and stuffed cushions with it, or used it in many other ways in their houses. But there wasn't all that much left around, really, as the fleece itself had to be taken off in one piece, rolled up with the fleece inside and the cut side outside, and put ready for the mill lorry which used to come over from the east, where the wool mills were, every two days while the shearing was going on.

The weather was good this particular year, and we only had two short sharp showers; even so, when it did rain it meant that we had to pack up for the time being, and shut the sheep waiting to be shorn into a stone-walled fold called a 'fank' until the rain had gone and we were able to start again.

Little diversions like this, though, were really a godsend to us, because we had time to rush to our homes and do something or other in the house which we had no time to do otherwise. My Shetlands came last, and Kirsty, Beth and I always did them. They had to be 'plucked', not shorn like the other sheep, and, strangely, they seemed to like it, for they stood perfectly still – even Billy, the ram – and sort of half dosed off to sleep while we were plucking them! Kirsty said she thought they were perhaps relieved, like the other sheep were after being shorn, to have thinner fleeces for the warmer months. The fleece of the Shetlands was naturally a 'moorit' colour – the brownish background to so many Fair Isle jumpers and cardigans.

Carol kept the stall open three days a week, so for the shearing she and Diarmid were able to come along and help us at Clachan. Fearchar had shown them both how to shear by hand, and they soon got quite quick at it. Now that electricity was coming to Clachan, however, we thought that this might be the last time we'd be shearing by hand. We supposed that after this we'd all be using clippers or shears, or whatever, run on the 'electrics' – and Kirsty didn't like the idea of it at all. And I wondered whether it would be so satisfactory in the long run, because when you did it by hand you were careful to clip off every bit you could. Well, that we would know when we'd tried them; one thing it would mean – we couldn't sit along the verges and do the job. It would have to be either near our own premises or in some communal place equipped with electricity. We didn't mind the latter, but we weren't keen to have numbers of sheep around the house, excepting my Shetlands which were more like pets, and never went very far from the house anyway. But there were only five of them.

While we were all carrying on with the good work Corrie, Tee-tee and Tòmas lay around with the crofters' dogs in various attitudes of repose, or sat up to have a grandstand view, as they preferred; evidently the trio took their cue from the crofters' dogs and kept their distance, not getting in the way at all. There were, of course, the odd times when somebody from each household would have to rush off to go and get the cows in, milk them and drive them back on to the brae, for this was a job which always had to be done twice daily. And while we were busy we could swallow a hunk of bread and cheese, which would keep us going until we knocked off at night. We had no time to cut sandwiches, and were far too tired at night to bother anyway! This was a time of hard work for us, but none of us minded it, really, and we all enjoyed the fun and wisecracks that flew around. We were also glad we were a long way from a main road for, as Kirsty said, if we'd been doing this job sitting along the main road, we'd have had the tourists queuing up with their cameras to take a snap of these disreputable-looking objects. We didn't put on anything but our very oldest things, of course, for a job like this.

They all owned blackfaced sheep but me, and I kept the wool from my sheep. I had about one and a half pounds of wool off a Shetland sheep because it was so fine and soft, but it went a long way when you knitted it up or used it for weaving, and you could spin it up to the fineness of a cobweb. The blackface fleece would on an average weigh about five pounds, but it was wiry and was used for carpets and rugs, not for cloth for garments. Blackface owners who wanted wool for knitting garments, or for weaving material that was going to be used for garments, used to buy the wool from people who had Cheviots, farther inland; Cheviots didn't do well in such exposed terrain as ours.

In mid-July, after we'd all been trying to catch up with chores and things which had had to be left over at shearing time, Jean came along one day to tell me that Sim had rung up from Rhinn and wanted to speak to me, so I walked back with her to the post office and got her to put me through. Sim was waiting at Angus's, as he and Flora weren't on the phone. Angus answered and called Sim to the phone, and Sim came to the point at once.

'Oh, Mistress Armstrong – ' he began hesitantly. 'It's about – Myrtle – '

'Goodness! Have you had an accident or – '

'No, no. I have to ask you if you want her back.'

'Anytime, Sim,' I replied, 'but you haven't had her long, have you? Hasn't she been satisfactory?'

'She certainly has, whateffer! But as you probably know, Flora doesna like Rhinn, and has been wanting to move back to Edinbro' for a longish time now. Well, she's had a letter from her brother, saying that there was a wee house for sale on the outskirts of the city near her parents, so we've said we'll take it. Flora knows the house and says it's very nice.' At this point he swallowed, and it struck me that poor Sim wasn't of the same mind as Flora, and would have preferred to stay in Rhinn with his friends at hand. Then he went on: 'Ourselves can move down there at once, so the removal men will be coming for the furniture on Friday.'

'So, of course, you won't be needing Myrtle any more – '

'Flora doesna wish me to take Myrtle to Edinbro'.'

I thought to myself that if Myrtle had been, instead of an Austin Seven, something about three times larger and twice as showy, Flora wouldn't have made any objection to her going to Edinburgh, too.

Then Sim went on: 'It's very sad I am to part with her, you must understand, but I promised yourself that if I *had* to part with Myrtle at any time I'd give yourself the chance to have her back if you wanted her – and, believe me, I'd far rather be keeping her.'

'Never mind, Sim. I quite understand – and I'd like to have Myrtle back. Thank you for remembering. When would you like me to come for her?'

'Well, I'd like to keep her to the very last, whateffer – '

'I'm sure you would. Well, I'll get someone to run me over on Friday before the removal men get there, if you like.'

'Ay – I'll chust *have* to part with her. I've taken care of her, and she looks fine – '

E

'I knew you'd take care of her, Sim. How much do you want for her?'

'I'd no' be wanting anything,' he assured me, 'but Flora says I *must* sell her.'

So I suggested ten pounds, which is what he gave me for her. No good trying to knock anything off for usage, because Flora would moan at the poor man for hours if I had. Sim was quite happy about the ten pounds so, saying I'd be over about ten-ish on Friday, I rang off. I'd be glad to have Myrtle in Clachan again, and if I couldn't do anything about getting her licensed just as present, seeing I had the other car, why worry? She'd be all right jacked up with a tarpaulin over her for the time being.

Carol's car was outside my house I saw as I was walking home, and she and Diarmid were waiting for me in the kitchen. They knew I wouldn't be long, because it was milking time. After greetings, Carol said, 'We've come to give you some news. Diarmid and I are engaged.'

'Oh, I *am* glad!' I cried – as though everyone hadn't guessed that already. We'd seen it coming on for some time! 'Congratulations! Is it "official"?'

'Oh,' said Diarmid, 'at Craig they had already guessed it! But you can't have some people knowing it officially and others not in a place like this, can you?' he grinned. 'So it's official as from tonight.'

'Won't Kirsty be excited!' I exclaimed. 'You'll go over and tell her tonight?'

'Oh, yes – we're going over now, and then we'll go on to see Jean; after that we'll have to speed back to Craig, because Diarmid's father's coming to dinner to celebrate the occasion,' Carol explained.

'And when's the happy day planned for?' I asked.

'Not just yet,' Carol replied for them both. 'Diarmid and I

think it'll be best to get all the coming events over first – the harvest, the hall opening, Kirsty's big "after-harvest" *ceilidh*, the closing for the winter months of the hotel and the hotel shop and the roadside stall – and, of course, getting the sheep down. Then everyone'll be able to breathe again, so we're going to be married in October.'

'A very nice month up here usually,' I said, 'and every likelihood of its being a fine day,' I added. 'And since you're so involved in all the doings of the lochside and Craig and Clachan, by October you'll be able to forget your worries and have a very nice honeymoon without having to worry if this and that are going on properly – '

'Yes, and Diarmid'll have taken over the job of looking after the estate too by October,' said Carol. 'The factor, Donald MacBean, is leaving in September – '

'And my father,' added Diarmid, 'said he could stay on until he was ready to go – to Canada. He's been very good, showing me what has to be done and seen to, and dealing with the office work attached to the job.'

'And both my uncle and Diarmid's father have offered us a piece of land on their estates to build a house on – '

'Jolly good!' I exclaimed, getting the sherry out of the cupboard. 'But isn't that a bit awkward?'

'Well, not so awkward as it might have been,' smiled Carol, 'because I've got such a lot to do here – and I mean to have that "selling-everything" shop I've spoken about one day, because it'll be such a boon to people. So I'll have to be within easy reach, and Diarmid'll be busy during the day, so it won't matter, you see? Diarmid's father is very understanding, too. He'll see our point, and if we build our house on that side of my uncle's land, it won't be far for either of them – and Aunt Annabel – to come to see us at any time.'

And after a few minutes' more chat, self having drunk to their health and happiness in sherry in lieu of champagne –

although whisky was generally used up here for these occasions – they left the car outside and trotted over to Kirsty's.

By the end of July, haymaking was in progress. The weather was good, and everybody started panicking to get their hay scythed and quoiled before the next shower came along. We rushed down umpteen times a day to quoil or un-quoil our hay, and when we did the latter we had to stop to spread it and toss it a bit. When a shower did come we'd rush down and quoil it again into a big one, so that it wouldn't get wet through. We usually scythed in the mornings, and, after spreading it two or three times, it was quoiled for nights. When the hay was ready to go into the barns it was imperative that this job was done on a fine day. A rope was laid along the ground and hay was piled on as much as you thought you'd be able to carry at a time. Then you tied it up with the rope and slung it on to your back – and from the rear you looked like a walking haystack with just your feet showing. Dumping it in the barn, you either went back for more hay or you did some more scything – and you did the house chores whenever you could!

The Friday I was to go over to Rhinn for Myrtle fell on one of these haymaking days, and with everyone so busy I was jibbing rather at asking someone to run me into Rhinn. The problem solved itself quite nattily because John thought he ought to go in to buy some nails, rope and other things from Angus, and Fearchar begged to come along because he too wanted things from Angus for his croft. Kirsty needed some groceries, and Fiona and John thought the ride would do the old lady good, so Kirsty came as well. And, of course, we took Blister with us – John's boxer dog. Blister was adorable. He was almost human. I swear he knew everything you said to him. Corrie was adorable, too, but whereas Corrie would wag his tail at a burglar, and would tie himself into a knot with emotion if you told him he was a good boy, Blister was made of different stuff, and might even put the wind up Flora if she tried on any tantrums so that voices were raised.

We went in the hotel brake, so all the passengers, and the goods too when purchased at Angus-the-Shop's, fitted into it a lot better than they would have done if our Myrtle had been the only car that could go.

We arrived at Rhinn about ten, and Kirsty and Fearchar walked along with me to Sim's house to say good-bye and good luck to them in their new home. Not that my two Clachan neighbours could stand Flora, but they thought it was the right thing to do, and nobody had anything against Sim, anyway. John would be walking along in a short time to say good-bye to Sim, then, Fearchar hoped, Blister would fix his bright eyes on Flora – and perhaps if she didn't like dogs, it'd make her want to get us all out of the way as soon as possible, which was what Fearchar and John wanted. But they needn't have feared. John had said that 'fear clutched at his heart every time he saw Flora', but Fearchar said you couldn't see much expression on her face anyway, because it was so plastered with cosmetics that you couldn't tell whether she was pleased or angry except by her voice, which, Fearchar maintained, was rather like a rasp. Anyway, here we were at the house, and I knocked on the door with my knuckles, since there was no doorknocker. Flora opened it, and Kirsty said she thought she frowned when she saw us, but couldn't be quite sure. . . .

Before I could get out: 'Good morning,' Flora burst out impatiently: 'Och – I thought it was the furniture van – '

'I'm afraid not,' I smiled, meaning to start off in a friendly way. 'I've come for Myrtle – '

'Myrtle!' she sniffed derisively. 'Fancy calling that car by a name!'

'But I must see Sim,' I told her. 'I have to have the logbook and insurance – '

'Sim!' Flora shouted, disdaining to answer me. He came hurrying in as though by magic. 'Go,' she ordered, 'and get whatever's wanted!'

'It's the logbook, Sim,' I said, 'and here are Kirsty and Fearchar. John's going to walk along in a minute. We all want to wish you and Flora happiness in your new home – '

'Ach – it's nice seeing you,' Sim exclaimed to my two companions as he shook hands with them. He looked round for Flora. He knew she had met Kirsty, but was going to introduce her to Fearchar. But Flora had gone. He stood a few moments chatting with them, then Flora called from the depths somewhere: 'Hurry and get what they want, Sim! And then come and tie up these books. The men'll be here at any minute now!'

Automatically he made his apologies to Kirsty and Fearchar and turned to go in when John came up with Blister. The front door was open and Blister went in to inspect, but very quickly came out again with Flora behind him wielding the broom. But on the doorstep he stood his ground and growled at her. 'Take your dog away!' she shouted angrily to John. John, livid, quietly called Blister to him, and we all felt the situation was saved. Sim chatted to John for another minute or two, Fearchar, Kirsty and I joining in; then Sim, in fear of his life, said he'd fetch the logbook and disappeared inside.

In a minute or two Sim came out, and we all walked round to Myrtle. She looked fine – well looked after, and shining with polish. Sim gave me the book, and I said we wouldn't detain him longer; handing him the envelope containing the ten pounds, I got in and drove out on to the road. The others said good-bye to Sim and told me they'd walk along to Angus's. Then I bid Sim good-bye – and Myrtle and I hurried away, out of the awkward atmosphere. We spent some time at the shop and got what we all wanted, and Fearchar said he'd drive back with me. Kirsty said she'd go back with John, so we started for home.

11

Opening day of the hall

After haymaking, when the hay was all stacked in the barns, life was more normal again for a while. Our days were busy, divided between the croft, the house, the byre and the hen-houses, but we were able to scrounge the odd half-hour in the evenings now, when we could get on with things we'd had to leave while the rush was on.

A couple of evenings after Myrtle came home I went along to Kirsty's for a brief chat and found Fearchar already well established in the armchair on the other side of the fireplace to Kirsty's, creating his usual Black Twist fog, and telling Kirsty how annoyed he was at Flora's bad behaviour when we went to Rhinn.

Carol, Beth and Seumas arrived soon after I did, and as usual we all pulled chairs up and crowded round Kirsty's perman-ently blazing fire – for although this was the beginning of August, every house kept a fire of sorts, even throughout the summer, as the fires up here were never allowed to go out. Except mine, that was, and sometimes Jean's. That, we were told, was because we didn't 'smoor' them properly, and per-haps we forgot the little prayer that the Gaels always say both when they smoor the fire at night, and when they stir it into a blaze in the morning. Jean and I confessed that sometimes we did, but, in actual fact, between Jean and myself – though tell it not in Gath – neither of us knew enough Gaelic to say a prayer of any sort in that language. Jean, however, was rectifying all that. She wasn't taken up doing croft-work when she wasn't busy in the post office, so she had begun some time ago to learn it from a primer she sent for, and with some help from Kirsty and Beth as to pronunciation. . . .

At Kirsty's that evening, Fearchar, having discussed the recent doings at Rhinn with Kirsty, resumed it again when we all arrived on the scene – starting off tactfully: 'It's myself who's glad indeed that Myrr-tle's back in Clachan.' He'd announced this in his megaphone voice to the room in general.

Carol said, 'How did you get on? John told Diarmid that Flora behaved very badly to Kirsty and Fearchar. John said too that the Highlanders always prided themselves on their good manners and courtesy as well as their hospitality, but that Flora didn't seem to possess any of these traits.'

'Ach no. But herself's no' a Highlander, Carol,' Seumas hurried to explain. 'We dinna care for folks that behaves like that, whateffer; but, you see, herself's no' a Highlander – '

'But folks *thinks* herself's a Highlander,' bawled Fearchar, 'and that's what ourselves are no liking much. Herself's coming from some place in the Lowlands, whateffer, and maybe some of the people there are no' so particular how they behave at all times!'

'You like Sim, though, don't you, Fearchar?' queried Beth.

'Indeed, yes,' he replied, 'and himself's a real Highlander, with nice manners whateffer – a kind mannie, too, is Sim. And he must have a terrible time with Flora tho' – '

'Herself puts too much of yon stuff on her face, whateffer,' remarked Beth. 'I wonder where she gets it? Angus is no' selling it – '

'Why do you want to know where she gets it?' her husband,

a strict elder of the church, asked her with a smirk. 'Are *you* thinkin' of using that stuff on your face too?'

'Ach, whisht, Seumas!' begged Beth, seeming to shrink into her shell.

Fearchar came to the rescue. 'But some of the tourists who come to the hotel, and who put it on their faces carefully, look very well, in spite of it! What's the matter there is that Flora puts it on with a putty knife!'

We all laughed, and Beth, joining in because she had to, came out of her shell again. 'Ach well – I'm certain whateffer,' she declared, 'that nobody's eyes ever looked like Flora's!'

'Does she make them up a lot?' Carol asked.

'Indeed herself does!' Fearchar shouted, grinning. 'Flora puts on that black stuff round her eyelashes, so they stick out, like little stalks – "cascara" it's called – '

'"Mascara", Fearchar,' corrected Beth, who liked to have things right. 'Well, Angus is no' selling it, so – perhaps she sends for it?'

'Maybe she does,' put in Kirsty, 'but I've known women who can't get hold of any to put on a mixture of vaseline and soot!'

'Ach, well, perhaps that's what herself does,' nodded Beth. 'I'd no' be putting anything past her, whateffer.'

Just at this point there was a diversion. Jean dashed in with a message for Carol. We were all pleased to see Jean, and, welcoming her, Kirsty offered to get a wee strupach for her in 'two tics'. But Jean said she wouldn't dare to leave the post office for longer than the time taken to pop along with Carol's message, much as she'd have loved to stay and join in with us all round the fire. 'I saw Carol's car outside,' she went on, 'so I knew where to find her. Fiona rang up. There's a berserk cow on the lochside road, and as you can't come home any other way, she says, it would be best to wait a little while before starting back. John and Hector have taken some rope and a stack-net, and they hope to get hold of the poor thing somehow – '

'Oh, I hope they won't get tossed or anything – '

'Don't worry about them, Carol,' went on Jean. 'Fiona says they've taken the brake, as I said, and that'll stand a good deal more buffeting than your car would. So you'll wait a little while, will you? I'll ring Fiona back and tell her you're here.'

Carol thanked her and asked Kirsty about 'berserk cows'.

'Well, usually they go like that when the calf's been taken away,' explained Kirsty. 'She'll be all right when she's tired herself out and has had some warm oatmeal and water in somebody's byre, and after a couple of days' rest she'll be able to be moved back to her own byre. They go sort of "mad" for the time being – '

'Oh, poor thing!' cried Carol.

Jean sped back to the post office, and Kirsty went on, 'If John and Hector can get hold of her, any crofter'll have her until herself's better, you see? They'll make room for her some-where, and just let her rest and give her food – and she'll be as right as rain in a few days' time. But you'll stay here – to give them a chance to catch her and take her in somewhere, Carol?'

'Yes, thank you, Kirsty,' she smiled. 'Fearchar, you seem very glad that Myrtle's back in Clachan!' grinned Carol. 'Are you very fond of the little car, then?'

'I am that!' he yelled. 'There's no wee car like Myrr-tle – and, do you know – she's never let Mistress Armstrong down! The only mishaps herself's had was no due to her engine or anything. When a spring broke it was on that very bad Craig-Fasach road, and when the king-pin was lost out o' her it was due to bad roads too. But never has any throuble been through her own fault, whateffer. Oh, ay, it's very fond of Myrr-tle I am – and did Lachlan and myself no' have a good bit to do with giving herself a good appearance?'

'Oh, yes,' I explained. 'Fearchar and Lachlan mended her
flapping mudguards and bonnet, Carol, and sprayed her body,
and I made her a new hood. You see, she had been in a farm-
yard. In fact, she was a hen roost!'

'My sainted aunt!' exclaimed Carol, which made everyone
laugh. 'I'd never in a hundred years have believed that! Kirsty!
Don't you think Fearchar and Lachlan – not forgetting her
owner, here – made a wonderful job of getting her to look
smart again?'

'Indeed, yes,' smiled Kirsty. 'Myrtle's worth her weight in
gold to Clachan.'

A fortnight later, Roddy's cow was back in circulation again.
John and Hector, the hotel barman, managed to capture it with
the help of the stack-net, and one of the lochside crofters took
it into his byre until it was better, and able to walk the five or
six miles back to its own.

We suppose that Flora and Sim got off according to schedule
to their house in Edinburgh, and we hope too that some kind
person showed Flora how to put on her make-up properly –
and also that she was never reduced to wearing vaseline-and-
soot-treated eyelashes. . . .

In Clachan we were in the middle of a rush again. We
gathered our turnips when we had the time, and we clamped
all but a few of them, which we put to store in the barns for
household use. The rest of the clamped turnips would be
stored over the winter for the animals.

The potatoes we also had to dig up when we had the time
but made the effort to get them all dug and sacked and into the
barns before we cut the corn. Several of us had three or more
acres of potatoes planted, which all had to be dug up by hand
for gathering, and every available minute had to be spent on
the job. By the time our potatoes were all in, what with
running up and down the steep croft to the potato ground,

and getting in our other work, too, I guess most of us must have lost a few pounds in weight! Several crofters who knew they'd have more of this crop than they'd need sacked their spare ones up and brought them up on a sled to the side of the track, where Carol and Diarmid would pick them up and take them along to sell at the stall. People were glad to get some money for their 'spares', for we all had this enormous 'autumn bill' in about now, when the Glasgow steamer brought the big boll sacks of meal, flour, and grain that would tide us over the winter. The grain in this case was used as we wanted, when we made scones, having ground down what we needed in the coffee grinder – by hand, of course.

Now, as the harvest panic was upon us, we all hoped fervently that the weather would be kind, for the sun would help so much in the drying. The oats had come up well, and most of us had good crops this year. On a warm and bright September morning someone from almost every house in Clachan, armed with a corran – a thin-bladed sickle – made their way to the part of their croft where the oats grew. Usually everyone tried to have a helper – two or more people if that was in any way possible – because there was a certain routine to be observed in carrying out the harvesting spree, and it was far more quickly done this way if three, or at any rate two, took part. Moira, the deaf-and-dumb girl, would come along and help any of us because she didn't grow oats herself, and she was more or less free for that time; Anna and Fearchar all worked their corn-cutting for half a day at a stretch, which left them free to go and help someone else with theirs. Not Kirsty, of course; she couldn't do the constant climbing up and down the croft brae now. Fearchar it was who came to help me, and I in turn went along to help him when he cut his oats. Alastair's boss gave him two days off work to cut the oats on his mother's croft, and both he and Anna, with Moira's help, should be able to break the back of their harvesting in the time.

The method of getting the oats cut in the shortest time was thus: the person with the corran cut an amount that would just about make a decent-sized bundle, which the second person, following close behind, picked up and bound round with a few twisted stalks of the oats. If there were a third person, this one took the bundle to the part of the croft where the stooks would be stood in groups of six bundles each, all propping each other up, with a piece of twine round the tops to keep them from being blown down by the wind. That was all there was to it really until the 'carrying', when you carried as many bundles to the barns as you could in one go – repeated over and over again – until your legs jibbed at climbing the croft brae and more with a heavy load on your back.

Several of us grew from two to four acres of oats, so you could reckon on our being nearly crippled by the time we'd carried all of that up to the barns! There were no mills up here at all, and transport cost too much to send it to be ground, so we used to keep separate whatever we wanted for smaller grain, for home use, and this we used as we wanted it. The rest was used, whole, for feeding the poultry.

Before we could grind it for household use we had to flail it. The flail consisted of two sturdy pieces of wood about eighteen inches long, joined by a piece of leather, but left loose enough for the flailing operation to be carried out. We spread a sheet on the barn floor when this had to be done, and laid down a 'bundle'. Then we beat the 'husks' end of the bundle with the flail, and afterwards sacked up the grain and stacked the stalks for straw.

Kirsty planned her *ceilidh* for the first week in October this year, as the 'grand opening' of the village hall was set for the Wednesday in the last week in September.

The hall was finished as regards the building of it by mid-September, and Carol and Catriona had been mad-busy whenever they could spare the time, decorating the inside of the place, and furnishing it as much as possible – getting the stove, cups and saucers and plates, and laying in a store of tea and sugar. They arranged for milk, scones and cakes to be brought along on the days when the hall was open. The chairs for the present would be borrowed from the Kirk, and as Carol had got together a number of films, a big screen was put up on one wall for showing them. If the people showed an interest in seeing films – which many of them had never had a chance to do before – the girls planned to join a film library so that they could hire films of plays and travel and documentaries for very little, to show on other occasions. Diarmid's father gave the screen and the film projector, and the Laird and Aunt Annabel had backed the project from the start, giving all sorts of things, for which the girls felt wholeheartedly grateful, as they hadn't got to wait for the money to come in before they could get on with things.

Now that the men had finished the alterations, the Laird and Aunt Annabel were very anxious that they should feel that all their hard work had not gone unappreciated – or unrewarded, for that matter – and they held a garden party at Craig House for those men and their wives and families one afternoon, a day or two before the opening. The catering was done by an Inverness firm, and various games and things to entertain the children were hired from somewhere else, and everyone enjoyed themselves, if laughter and happy faces were anything to go by. But that wasn't all. The Laird, thoughtful soul that he was, had an envelope ready to give every man of them as he was leaving, and the envelope contained twenty pounds towards the frightful 'autumn bill' that everybody dreaded.

The Wednesday of the 'grand opening' of the hall arrived, and it was a beautiful day. Those with cars ferried people to and from the hall; anyone who wanted a lift was to let Jean-Post-Office know as she had a list of the cars available and arranged which car was going to take whom, and at what time. The real opening was at four o'clock, and as the Laird performed the opening ceremony, he added that there was to be a surprise that afternoon; the only people in the secret were the Laird himself, Aunt Annabel, Carol and Catriona, and all of them had been sworn to secrecy.

Time was going on and everyone wondered what the surprise was. The Laird and Aunt Annabel and the girls helped to take the tea and cakes round, chatting to everyone, and telling them what was involved in taking whatever classes any of them *wanted* to take.

Carol had been typing in every spare minute for weeks, and now she had leaflets on whatever subject a person was interested in, and if they referred to the leaflet, Carol told them, it would help them to understand the methods of doing things. She had also got out a couple of hundred lists of subjects and dates of their classes. Diarmid had made a splendid notice board – an essential for the hall. And the Laird said at the opening that he was very anxious to have some competitions in the categories of baking and bottling, and more competitions for the best crops of certain kinds, and for garden flowers and wild flowers. Then there would be demonstrations – the first one, at the next meeting, would be taken by Catriona and Beth, on dyeing with wild plants – always an interesting subject.

At five there was to be a changeover, when people who were standing in for other people would be fetched down to the hall, and the others were taken back. At 4.45 on the dot, the Laird's surprise materialized. . . .

12

Return of Trudy and Dugald

The Laird had by this time managed to make his way through the crush of people to a spot near the door, Aunt Annabel following closely in his wake, where they stood talking to Iain-the-Police and Fearchar. Suddenly Iain happened to glance towards the road, and there stood a brand-new bus – bigger than a mini-bus, but much smaller than a coach. He was just going to draw the others' attention to it when out of it stepped Trudy, my niece, and her husband, Dugald. They were both over from America for a short holiday.

This was a tremendous surprise to everyone, and it couldn't have been a better one, for Dugald had been popular with all the crofters and their wives ever since he was a little boy playing with their own little boys, and committing all the crimes that other small boys of the time and place committed. The worst of these was fishing on the Sabbath, and Dugald, treated exactly the same as all the other small boys, was on several occasions caught at his Sunday fishing, and paraded off by the ear to his father, the Laird. Trudy seems to have won people's hearts, too, and it was a sad day for the communities of our loch when the newlyweds decided to go and live, temporarily, at any rate, in America, so that Dugald could put a property inherited by his father on its feet.

So suddenly seeing the couple again was overwhelming, and as they walked down the path to the hall they were quickly surrounded, and engaged for some time on answering question after question from all their old friends.

The Laird had told them over the phone to America of the three important coming events and gave them the dates, and they managed to fly over now, so that they'd be at the hall on the opening day, and be able to go to Kirsty's harvest *ceilidh* and to the wedding of Carol and Diarmid – Diarmid having been a very old friend of Dugald's.

'So we managed to get here by 4.45,' smiled Trudy, 'as you wished, Father-in-law, and so that we'd be able to see the people who were leaving at five o'clock to take over from the others left to 'mind' things, when the people ferrying them to and fro with their cars would bring the others back.' By keeping to the Laird's arrangement, the couple would have met everyone today sometime.

'And the bus?' asked everybody. 'What's the bus doing here?'

'It's your bus,' laughed Dugald. 'The Laird asked us to pick it up at Inverness and bring it along. It's a present to you all from him.' And everyone, surprised but excitedly happy, trooped out to inspect their new gift.

Trudy was introduced to Carol by Catriona, who was wild with excitement at seeing Trudy again. They had been great friends when Trudy had been staying with me for a three-month holiday at the hotel when I was down there. They joined Dugald, John's great friend, and Fiona. Carol was the odd one out at the moment as the others were good friends, but she was dragged into the fold right away, and made to feel one of them.

Inside the hall, chatting over tea and cakes was still going on, and Catriona thought that now it might be a good time to show the films, so Carol went and stood beside the projector, and the Laird announced that now Carol's films would be shown on the screen, and that if people liked the idea she could hire plays and things to show.

They laughed a lot at some of them, where people recognized themselves doing this and that, and in the films of cows and other croft animals, they were all kept very busy recognizing which animal belonged to whom. They liked the filming so much that when the Laird took a count of hands as to whether they'd like Carol to hire the other films he'd spoken about, the vote for her to do that was unanimous. When it was time to go home John was able to get all the Clachan people into the bus, and he drove them right to their doors. The other people were ferried in various cars, and at the end the Laird and Aunt Annabel went home in the Daimler. After clearing up, all the young people retired just down the road to the hotel. Fiona and Trudy had much to say to each other, and as Carol and Trudy, Diarmid and Dugald felt they should go back soon to Craig House, they arranged to have a longer session at the hotel the following night.

It had all been a most exciting day for everyone, and quite a number of people didn't sleep too well that night – living it all over again. . . .

Trudy and Dugald were over for a holiday of just over three weeks, as Dugald couldn't leave his business for a longer period at present. They suggested that Carol and Diarmid should come back to the States with them, using their home as a base to go off to different places of interest from there. They would be returning to Craig about mid-November, but their house wouldn't be ready for them by then, so they planned to stay at Craig House until it was.

The 'harvest *ceilidh*' which Kirsty always threw was one of the great events at Clachan, and nobody would miss it if they could help it for anything. It took place as planned, during the first week in October, about a week before the wedding. Fearchar was in great form that night and told several stories which, although everyone had heard them before, commanded a silence throughout the whole company, and you could have heard a pin drop. He was, of course, accompanied by his pipe and clouds of smoke.

Kirsty, Anna and Beth must have spent hours and hours baking, for the big table in the kitchen was simply groaning with food. Kirsty had wanted everyone to come who could; they took her at her word, and the company overflowed from the kitchen into the hall and the porch. There weren't nearly enough chairs and stools, as one would expect, and upside-down buckets with a cushion or a folded coat on top came into use; nobody bothered over things like that, and everyone was determined to enjoy themselves as they always did at Kirsty's.

Kirsty announced to us all when everyone had arrived that this *ceilidh* was partly to celebrate the end of a successful harvest, as usual, but it was also to celebrate the engagement of Carol and Diarmid. Healths would be drunk later, she said, but for the moment the girls would be handing round the tea and scones, cakes, and chicken sandwiches, for which, she smiled, amidst terrific applause, she herself had made the bread. Trudy and Dugald came along with Fiona and John, who had managed to come together, because the hotel had just closed for the winter, and we were all so delighted that Jean-Post-Office had taken her day off for that particular day so that she could join us, too.

The *ceilidh* took its usual form: after the tea and sandwiches etc. while everyone chatted loudly to each other and an awful din went on, in which it was imperative to shout yourself or you wouldn't have been heard, Fearchar's several legends followed. Everyone listened almost with bated breath, and never minded that he'd told them umpteen times before. But Beth perhaps listened more carefully than anybody else, because she was ready, if Fearchar left any detail out, to rush in to remind him – caring not one whit about the angry expression Fearchar shot at her for her trouble.

Then followed lots of the old working songs, some of them in Gaelic. These some of us could only hum to, but we all joined in those in English, or Scottish, rather, for we could cope with that. Catriona led off the singing with gusto, and everyone joined in lustily. The noise was terrific, and they must have heard it almost as far away as the Hebrides.

When Kirsty thought there'd been enough singing, she announced that the girls were bringing in her famous Athol Brose for everyone to drink the health of Carol and Diarmid – and everyone did, many preferring to be certain their good wishes were genuine enough by having a couple of glasses or cups of it then, though we all knew Kirsty always kept strictly to her routine of giving everyone some Athol Brose before they left the hospitality of her house.

It was well on into the next morning when the last guests departed, so Fearchar told us, for he was one of them; the girls stood by the door with jugs of Athol Brose for everyone to have as they left. It had been a wonderfully happy evening, as all Kirsty's *ceilidhs* were.

And everyone was only barely back to normal again when, a week later, it was the date of the wedding. . . .

13

The wedding

The day before the wedding was a fine, bright October day, and everyone hoped it would be like this tomorrow. Carol was still a little disappointed that there wouldn't be any music at her wedding. She couldn't really imagine what a wedding service would be like without any! Aunt Annabel was sympathetic, because she'd offered several times to make the Kirk a gift of an organ, but when the minister had put it to the elders of the Kirk, they told him that the people wouldn't agree to it, because any musical instrument inside a church was regarded as an instrument of the Devil.

'So, my dear,' said Aunt Annabel, 'there's no way round this unless somebody agrees to play the music *outside* the Kirk, I'm afraid, and I don't know how that can be done here.'

'It's just that the music mustn't actually be *played* inside the church?' asked Carol. Her aunt nodded.

'The younger people have gone off to the towns for the most part, you see, Carol,' she explained, 'and this has left only the older ones – and they all stick close to the old ideas.'

Carol went along to consult Fearchar about it. He was one of the elders besides being the Precentor, and Carol's request put him in a spot. He liked Carol and would most surely have given in himself, because she had done so much up here to benefit everyone and he thought they owed it to her. But he knew the opposition would be so fierce that he couldn't face the extremely strict congregation and say that he would defy them, and allow Carol to have music in the church. Carol's heart crashed to her shoes and she said nothing, but Fearchar made up his mind to compromise.

'Look you, Carol,' he told her confidentially, 'ourselves'll borrow the gramophone from the hall, and there's hundreds of records there as well – and amongst that lot we ought to find some of the sort of music you want for a wedding service, for all Fiona and John's friends turned them out for the hall – all sorts. . . . There chust must be a piece yourself'll like – '

Carol felt much better at once. 'Then what are we waiting for, Fearchar? Let's go along, shall we, and see what we can find.'

'And I'd be thinkin' that nobody can make any objections if the gramophone's stood on a table outside,' Fearchar remarked.

So they went straightaway along to the hall and rummaged through hundreds of records, finding three of them that would do fine, Carol said. One was 'the Voice that breath'd o'er Eden', and another was a wedding march, and, trying a few pieces of music, they decided on a quiet, very nice piece that would do very well, Carol thought, to play when the people were walking into the church. Fearchar had operated the gramophone before and agreed to play it for her wedding. . . .

The wedding the next day was to be at twelve o'clock to give people time to get there from places far afield, and for those who would have to come long distances by boat. The weather was just what had been hoped for – warm and sunny and with scarcely – wonder of wonders! – a breath of wind! The church couldn't hold all those who came, and a great many people stayed outside and stood near the church windows, which were opened so that they could hear the service. Fearchar stood beside a small table which held the gramophone and several records in a small heap, placed in order by John before the ceremony began, so that Fearchar would only have to put each on to the turntable as John gave him a sign from a window. Nothing could go wrong. . . .

That's what they thought.

When the trouble had started Carol and Diarmid had been standing before the minister with the Laird on one side – he gave Carol away – and John, the best man, on the other. Carol looked really beautiful in her long, white, satin wedding dress and veil of Honiton lace, with flowers sent specially from Glasgow by train and rushed to Craig House in time for the wedding. Diarmid looked fine, too. His build was just right for the kilt, and the two of them made – so everyone thought – a most handsome couple.

And all went well until some of the dogs which accompanied the crofters wherever they went – to church as well – spotted the dog of a crofter from some miles away which they didn't know; and then the trouble began. First one and then another set on the newcomer, and that was the start of such a row that the minister had to stop the service for a minute, which bothered Diarmid, feeling nervous, but made Carol giggle, which she tried hard to hide.

Men got up and grabbed their dogs as soon as the fight began, if they could, but some could not. Seumas, as principal elder, thought the only solution was to drive the fight out of doors, which they managed to do. He broke off a rowan twig and, laying about the dogs with it, he managed in the end to stop the fight. But unfortunately, in the mêlée, the records got knocked off the table; although Fearchar held on to the gramophone itself for dear life, he forgot where he was for the minute and brought his best megaphone voice into play, swearing loudly as the records fell to the ground.

The first round had gone off well, for when John had made

the sign at the window for the music to begin for the bridal procession to walk up the aisle, Fearchar carried the order out in an excellent manner, and turned the music off again when John gave him another sign. The latter was kept busy, as he also had to carry out his duties as best man. After the ring had been put on Carol's finger and the couple had been pronounced man and wife, he had to dash to the window with the next signal. This was for the hymn: 'The voice that breath'd o'er Eden', and only a few minutes earlier due to the dog-fight and the records being dropped, and not having been put back in their right order, John was horrified to hear the strains of 'Sleep thy last sleep, free from care and sorrow'.

Frantically, he gave the sign to turn the music off, and Fearchar, doing as he was told, looked hurt because to him, so long as it was music, it was all right – and he wouldn't know the difference between one hymn and another because up here they sang psalms, not hymns.

Fearchar now began looking for the record of the wedding march. This music was bound to be right, he thought, and there was only one of a wedding march. But it couldn't be found for some time. Then one of the men found it in pieces by the church wall. It had been stamped upon!

Well, thought Fearchar, they must have music to walk out to or Carol will be upset. . . . So in desperation he put on just *any* record, so long, he decided, as it was music – and the bride and groom walked down the aisle to the porch to jazz music. . . .

The reception, held in the grounds of Craig House, went off well, and when the time came for the couple to depart for their honeymoon, Seumas drove them to a hotel in Inverness where they were going to stay the night, in order to catch an early train to London the next morning. Here they were going to stay for a week, and then go on to Southampton, where Trudy and Dugald would meet them, and the four young people would then board a liner for New York. At New York

Dugald would pick up his car and drive them all to his and
Trudy's home about a hundred miles away from the city.
Using this address as a base, Carol and Diarmid would be able
to go off to places of interest, and in the second week in
November Trudy and Dugald would be seeing Carol and
Diarmid off by liner again for Southampton, to arrive back
finally at Craig in the beginning of December. Even then,
Diarmid was worried in case the snow, which they'd heard
had already fallen in the Scottish Highlands, would be too
deep in the passes for them to get through– but this proved not
to be the case, and they reached Craig safely, after having been
met at the railway station in Inverness by the Laird and Aunt
Annabel.

Clachan, Craig and the lochside were all glad that Carol and
Diarmid would be returning to live in the neighbourhood
permanently. Carol had so obviously had the one thought in
mind all the time – would this or that be of any use in helping
the people to have things a bit more easy to cope with? She
had been the means of pin money coming to them, and, never
having had money on the side before, the crofters' wives
especially were delighted. The money they made was enough
for a few luxuries from the mail order firm, and Carol was
pleased for them. She had thrown herself into the village hall
project wholeheartedly, and it had been a great success – and
a great boon, too, to those crofters' wives who would never
have been able to spare the time to cope with all the compli-
cations of a trip to Inverness, or even to get to Rhinn for some
of the necessities. Even if they had, that would only be for the
shopping, whereas the hall brought them all so much pleasure
in one way and another, and they had come to look forward
to its days of opening.
    Now, and to the front, not the back of her mind, was the
idea of having a shop like Angus's; a shop nearby would be

very much welcomed by all the Clachanites, and those from the other lochside communities, too. Carol hoped to get the shop started by June. Kirsty said it would be lovely having it, for the summer months were so busy, and there the shop would be, and you wouldn't have to do without something you wanted urgently until someone was going where they could get whatever you wanted!

Yes, there was no doubt in the minds of the Clachan people that Carol was a wonderful girl. Catriona was, too, but with the school to keep her so busy she hadn't the opportunity to put in the amount of time that Carol had to get on with a project.

The snow was early in coming this year, not that we ever had it very deep round about the crofts, but only up in the nearby mountains. But what happened was that snow blocked the passes about twenty miles inland and on from there, and there was no other way of reaching the towns. The drifts were always at the very least three-quarters of a mile long, and often much more, and we got nothing, even mail or medical supplies, for several months, unless they were brought if the sea wasn't too rough, once every few weeks. The gales from now on until about April were often about 100 miles an hour around the coasts up this way.

The birds had all practically gone – barring the gulls, the occasional eagle and, fairly frequently, buzzards. The hoody crows and a few other small birds were, with the gulls, all that were left us throughout the winter months. At the end of October the wedges of geese had flown over us on their way to their winter feeding grounds – some a bit earlier, in fact. Tiny red-brown field mice found their way into our houses if it was very stormy and cold, and although the men had no hesitation in killing them, and though they would have it that they were ordinary vermin, we women found them far too attractive to hurt – and they'd go again as soon as the weather got better. Never more than one or two would come into any house, so there wasn't much to make a fuss about!

Our croft gates were left open now, and the sheep had been driven down, away from the drifts, so they, together with the deer, wild goats, Highland cattle and anything else on four legs that felt like it, it always seemed, found their way into our crofts.

Christmas was like an ordinary day here, and people went off to work the same as on any other day – although Kirsty always asked anybody to her house if they were visitors, and did her best to give them a Christmas dinner – with chicken instead of turkey, for we had no turkeys up this way. Hogmanay was the great time up here, as in any other part of Scotland, and on New Year's Eve the men would go round to all the houses with a 'bottlie', and those visited would join them in a drink to health and happiness in the coming year, and they would receive a drink in exchange – always whisky up here.

Throughout the worst months the animals and poultry had to be cared for just the same, but under more difficult conditions, and the cows were always kept in during the coldest spells, and on some days we had to keep the poultry in, too, or they'd have been blown into the loch!

Fearchar each year made fathoms and fathoms of heather rope – we went nautical here over rope measurements! – bringing a length round to each house about the beginning of November. Big stones were fastened to each end of the rope, and these weighted lengths were thrown over the tops of the roofs to keep them on in the winter gales.

From about the end of September onwards we had the most beautiful spectacles in the sky each night – the aurora – and everyone, even the Clachanites who didn't appear to think lots of things were as wonderful as we liked to think they were, enjoyed watching the aurora. These spectacles took different forms, and all were fantastically colourful and animated.

January came and went – and February. Snow still blocked the passes, and we pottered around our byres and yards where the croft animals and poultry were now, and paid visits to each other's houses accompanied by our knitting. And regarding knitting, we really got through a tremendous amount of it in the winter for stocking the hotel shop. Jumpers and cardigans – especially those patterned with Fair Isle designs – sold well to the summer tourists, and it all put money into the croft kitties, which many crofters' wives could do with. Transport of any-thing from the towns that you wanted cost so much in the ordinary way, that although, apart from the big autumn bill, there were few other expenses during the winter. This bill was such a large proportion of the average crofter's money that anything gained by knitting, weaving or by selling their sur-plus produce was very welcome.

Before we realized it, we were round to April again. The roads were clear and the mails were getting through normally once more. And before the end of the month we were in the thick of having 'the electrics' connected to every house, whether we wanted it or no. Kirsty was still annoyed about it, but most other people, taking the cue from some of the loch-side people who had had it for some time, thought how nice it would be to own fridges, electric irons and electric kettles, even if they had to buy them from the 'electrics' people on the never-never. . . .

Both the peewits' storm and the lambing time were with us again and another year at Clachan was beginning for me. It was always, once I'd come here to live, the only place in the world for me – the people, the scenery and the peace and quiet of the mountains and loch meant – and always will do – everything to me, and I fervently hoped that the place would

remain as it was for many more years without being spoilt
by modernization, and the thoughtless kind of tourists who
leave litter around. And actually, I couldn't believe that
Clachan ever *would* alter – so long as Kirsty had her way and
insisted upon the track being left in its appalling condition.
And may Kirsty have her way about that track for many years
yet. . . .

St. John's Wort